THE JAGUARS THAT PROWL OUR DREAMS

The Jaguars That Prowl Our Dreams

New and Selected Poems

1974 – 2018

Mary Mackey

With an Introduction
by D. Nurkse

Marsh Hawk Press

2018

ISBN: 978–0–996–99112–4

First Edition 10 9 8 7 6 5 4 3 2 1

Marsh Hawk Press books are published by Marsh Hawk Press, Inc.,
a not-for-profit corporation under section 501 (c) 3 United States Internal Revenue Code.

Cover & author photos by Angus Wright

Book design by Heather Wood
www.heatherwoodbooks.com

The text for this book is set in Berling Roman.

Library of Congress Cataloging-in-Publication Data
Mackey, Mary, author.
The jaguars that prowl our dreams: new and selected poems, 1974 – 2018 / Mary Mackey.
First edition. | East Rockaway: Marsh Hawk Press, 2018. | Includes bibliographical references.
LCCN 2018009168 | ISBN 9780996991124 (pbk.)
LCC PS3563.A3165 A6 2018 | DDC 811/.54—dc23
LC record available at https://lccn.loc.gov/2018009168

Marsh Hawk Press
P.O. Box 206, East Rockaway, NY 11518-0206
www.marshhawkpress.org

— for —
A.W.

Contents

Infinite Worlds

PART TWO *Selected Poems 1974–2014*

Travelers With No Ticket Home (2014)

Preface

The poems in this collection span over four decades including a handful written as early as 1968 and forty-seven new poems written between 2014 and 2018. Such a long journey deserves a map. Part One contains all the new poems, divided into two sections. *The Culling* comprises twenty-one poems set in Western Kentucky that evoke a clannish, rural way of life that has virtually disappeared since 1975 when I last observed it firsthand. *Infinite Worlds* contains twenty-six new poems that vary widely in theme, location, and intent linked by an exploration of the the tropical jungle outside us and within us, plus a surreal and sometimes hallucinatory appreciation of the visionary power of fever.

Part Two contains selected poems from my seven previously published collections. All appear appear in chronological order beginning with poems from the earliest years of the Women's Movement written from 1968 to 1973 and first published in *Split Ends* (1974) and ending with poems from *Sugar Zone* (2011) and *Travelers With No Ticket Home* (2014). The only exceptions are the five poems which comprise the introductory section entitled *A Threatening Letter to Shakespeare*. Although these poems were written over a period of thirteen years from 1974 to 1987, they clearly belong together. In theme and intent, Juliet speaks to Ophelia; Ophelia speaks to Desdemona; Desdemona speaks to Cleopatra; and at our peril, we all speak and are spoken to by Lady Macbeth.

Although some of the more recent poems in Part Two contain Portuguese words and phrases, the English-only portions are complete poems in themselves. They stand alone and can be read as if they were written solely in English.

I am not the same poet nor in many ways even the same person as the woman who wrote some of these poems over forty years ago, but with a few exceptions, I have resisted the urge to revise them, limiting myself to the correction of minor errors left over from the days when proofreaders used a blue pencil and a spell check involved thumbing through an unabridged dictionary.

—M. M.

Introduction

by D. Nurkse

"Days and months are travelers of eternity," said Basho, set-
ting out on a last expedition. In *The Jaguars That Prowl Our
Dreams*, a breathtaking "new and selected," Mary Mackey,
quintessential traveler, takes the reader to fascinating places:
rural Kentucky, the Amazon, Yucatan, New York, California,
ancient Japan, "a nice room with a view of the Taal volcano."
Always she's alive to estrangement, "the trance of the south."
She's a traveler hip enough to know there's always another
layer of the unknowable between her and her surroundings,
however skillfully she decodes them — see the poem "Defec-
tive Instructions for Becoming a Shaman."

Mackey, like Basho, is also traveling in time. She follows
the arc of a lifetime, as you might follow the left bank of the
Orinoco, thrilling to the strangeness of human identity as it
comes to know itself, as it casts itself into a lover's eyes, or a
strangers, or a cat's. Mackey's lines are brilliantly honed to the
visceral, playful, savage detail or epigram. Army ants make
"their dead into bridges," a woman in the wilderness twists
her wedding ring into a fish hook and survives, a mother
"taught me compassion because / she could not feel it."

But behind the compelling surfaces, transcendental back
stories assemble themselves: the self-creation of a psyche over

generations; the hidden history of an era, from the flowering of feminism through the endless death agony of the patriarchy; a blunt story of love in struggle, struggle in love, triumph and dispossession. As in the poem "Witness," there's a knack for exploring the horrific without rhetoric, without playing the disaster card. Always Mackey's eye is drawn to the marginalized, the poor, the outcast, the trivialized, the ones who stand at the center of the human adventure.

The Jaguars That Prowl Our Dreams is a dangerous and fortunate journey. Mary Mackey has created an oeuvre, wilder, more open to change with each passing year. Hers is a monumental achievement.

PART ONE

New Poems

THE CULLING

Whenever I Feel Like Complaining

I remember my Great Aunt Ebbie
who 3 days before she turned 76
hand-shucked 40 acres of corn
after it was beaten down by a
hail storm

standing on one leg
because the other
had been eaten off
by a hog

which also had also eaten
off one of her arms
meaning she did it
one-legged and
one-handed
in the pouring rain

Et

dialectal past tense and past participle of eat
Middle English *eten*, from Old English *etan*
akin to Old High German *ezzan* to eat,
Latin *edere*, Greek *edmenai*

your Great Aunt Ebbie has suffered a farm accident
my mother says

what she means my father says
is that a hog et your Aunt Ebbie.

et all of her? I ask

no, just her left leg
and part of her right arm

think she'll live?

I expect so
those Walker girls
are tough

John! my mother screams
how can you stand there
and talk about this to Mary
as if it's normal

While Listening to Pinchas Zukerman Play Mozart

couldn't you at least
have said "eaten"
my mother whispers

you're a doctor
a well-educated man

no one
ever says someone
was "eaten" by hogs
my father whispers
they are "et"
it's the only possible word

I cannot   whispers my mother
turning pale
cannot stand for . . .
cannot bear to . . .

my mother never finished that sentence
so we never knew if it was
the grammar
or the hogs
that bothered her
most

I Prove I Am My Mother's Daughter

my great aunt has suffered
a farm accident
I told my Harvard
roommates

she had a . . .

fall

Why My Mother Gave Up Pork Forever

for Christmas
they sent us

the ham

The Day the Hogs Ate Aunt Ebbie

Only one ornery old sow really
but the story gets better in the telling:

how at the age of 73 Aunt E went out
to the pigpen to slop the hogs
and stepped on a shoat that squealed
like it was being baconed alive

how a two hundred pound cross-eyed sow
milk-titted and crazed with mother lust
charged her   knocked her down
planted its muddy hooves on her chest
crunched her legbones like breadsticks
ate off her arm
and would have had her head and heart too
if Aunt Kitty thin as a willow
and 80 if she was a day
hadn't come barreling out of the kitchen
with a broom and beat the beast off Ebbie
like she was pounding a pig carpet

Some say in that terrible hour
Kitty called on Jesus to give her strength
others insist she swore like a mule skinner

"hang on, honey!" Aunt Kitty yelled
as she jammed the broomstick
down the sow's throat
"you still got one good leg   and this old bitch
is headed for ham"

Jesus on a Scarf

my people weren't religious
they went to church on Sunday
mostly for the company
to learn the going price for shoats
and grab a funeral parlor fan or two
for when the weather turned hot come August.

the only praying I ever heard about was when
the hog ate off Aunt Ebbie's leg
and she sent away to a radio preacher
for a magic scarf
with the face of Jesus on it
that was supposed to make it grow back.

she tried the Jesus scarf for a while with no results
sent her artificial leg out
to have the spring in the knee readjusted
and gave up on God.

Kin

We were related to everybody in Hamilton County
literally everybody
judges and lawyers and county clerks
and barbers and druggists and soda jerks
and moonshiners and farmers and ferry boat captains
and the rich people in the big white houses
and the poor ones down by the slough

Total strangers would come up
as soon as they saw you on the street
throw their arms around you and say
my great-grandma is buried next to your great-grandma
or I'm your cousin 17 times removed on your third uncle's side

or
my   my   my   you look just like your daddy
has he ever got out of prison?

How They Got Here

in steerage
so hungry they ate the green slime
off the walls of the hold

indentured
grubbing the burdock out of the corn
with short-handled hoes
sucking on stones   chewing weeds
sleeping with the cattle

sometimes when a tired, red-knuckled
woman turned toward a man   he caught in her
face a glimpse of the bruised beauty
of a winter sunset

on the day they finally bought their freedom
burned their indentures
and left the coast of Virginia behind
to follow Mr. Boone through the Gap
their only possessions were
five wool blankets   three bags of flour
half a pound of salt two iron skillets
an axe   and a small leather bag
	half-filled with seed corn

The Culling

they buried their babies and mourned for them
buried children who died of typhoid and measles
and blood poisoning from stepping on rusty nails
and lock jaw, tetanus and diphtheria and whooping cough
and God knows what
young women who died in childbirth and young men
who died in farm accidents and drowned in rivers
were cut to pieces by bailing wire, run over by harrows
kicked by mules and crushed by tractors

they had funerals when there was not enough of a man
left to put in a coffin
not enough left of a woman to put in the ground
ghost funerals for people who disappeared in the river
whose bodies never floated up in the shallows

afterwards
they went back to the farm
milked the cows
fed the chickens

cows   Aunt Ebbie said
don't care if you've just come from a funeral
wearing your best Sunday black go-to-meeting dress
or just come out of the kitchen wearing
a calico housedress and a feedsack apron

chickens don't care if you're sad or happy
you have to feed them
you have to feed them every day
they don't know what's happened
they don't care what's happening
you're not gonna get much sympathy from cows
and you'll never get no sympathy from chickens.

Great-Grandfather Horace Ebenezer Wanted Boys

but God didn't come through
so he gave all his daughters boys' names
Aunt Christopher and Aunt Ebenezer and Aunt Fenwick

when Ida Alice   the youngest   was born
he gave up and saddled her with two old maids' names
saying:

no one's gonna marry into a family of girls

Hands

Great-Grandfather Horace Ebenezer
stalked around the farm
in a white suit
overseeing the hired hands
who were mostly a florid -faced
heavyset guy named
Fatty

Fatty (self-named)
lived rent-free in a little cabin
on the edge of the farm
near the bottoms

people said Fatty was so dumb
he killed his own baby
by putting it out on a snow bank
when it had measles
to bring down its fever

but they also acknowledged
Fatty
made the best knives
in Hamilton County

Fatty Made Knives Out of Crosscut Saw Blades

sharp   precise   treasured
passed down through the generations
with hand carved handles

since he couldn't read
he took them to Aunt Ebbie
who burned his name on them
with the tip of a hot poker

Fatty gave his knives away for free
never taking money

proud that he could do something better than anyone else
proud he could grind steel
chop wood
cut through things

Disaster Tourism

drive us around
says Aunt Kitty
we don't get out much

see that farm to your left
crying shame
fools sold it to Peabody Coal
all the topsoil stripped off
those folks never gonna get a crop of corn
worth spit again
if they live to be a hundred

see that tumble down shack
that's where Mr. Joe Brady
took an axe to his wife
knocked her on the head
with the blunt end
then chopped her up in 4 neat
pieces with the blade
and tried to feed her
to his hogs

they wouldn't eat her
says Aunt Ebbie
Mabelle Brady was too mean
a woman even for hogs

when did all this happen

'84 or there about says Aunt Kitty
Nah says Aunt Ebbie
year of the flood
and the Whiskey Rebellion
1792, late spring

drive on honey says Aunt Kitty
see that place yonder
last man hanged in Hamilton county
lived there
gave his soul to Jesus at the camp meeting
less than a month later
danced on air like a backslidden Baptist

man was saved just in the nick of time

How My First Husband Ended Up
Wearing a Black Fur Coat
with a White Stripe Down the Back

when I got divorced

my sweet Kentucky grandmother
who didn't even have the heart
to kill a chicken
said to me
somebody better sit
with his back to the wall

Divorce Kentucky Style

want me to shoot him
my brother asked

god no
it's bad karma
you don't have gun
we don't live in Kentucky
and I'm a semi vegetarian
who doesn't eat things
with lips

Rules of Engagement

if a strange man comes to the door
when you're alone in the house
greet him with a shotgun
and don't lower the barrel
until he claims kin

when he claims kin
he'll tell you who he's related to
if you don't recognize the names
back for at least 3 generations
turn him away

if he asks where your neighbors live
say you never heard of them
if asks how to get somewhere
send him in the wrong direction

never kill a garter snake
never steal pennies off the eyes
of a corpse

when sharing your favorite recipe
always leave out one ingredient

The Long Black Veil Rule

if you're sleeping with a married woman
you can't tell anyone
even if keeping the affair a secret
costs you your life

there are no illegitimate children
in Kentucky
only widows
orphans
and dead men

For Twelve Generations We Hated the Colbys

the Colbys were bad   evil   full of meanness
every time one of our people fell sick
the Colbys came out and paced our fence lines
figuring to buy our land cheap
before the corpse was cold

when Aunt Kitty married a Colby
things fell apart like Shakespeare's
Romeo and Juliet
only with shotguns.

Aunt Kitty's husband Mr. Colby
took her to Detroit
where he went to college and got an education

when the two came back
the Colbys dove them off the place
and wrote them out of the will
and Aunt Kitty and her husband
had to go sharecrop in Henderson

When the Last Walker Girl Died

when the last Walker girl died
and was put in the family graveyard
the Colbys finally got our farm.

they tore down the house
they tore down the chicken coops
they tore down the barn and the shed
and the smokehouse where hams had been smoked
and taken down to New Orleans on flat boats.

they pulled up the stones that had the names
of the uncles who had drowned in the Colorado Gold Rush
carved on them chopped down the orchard
and took a bush hog to the blackberry vines

the Colbys planted corn   long green rows
greener where our hogs had wallowed
greener where our chickens had scratched
corn   corn   as far as you could see
rows and rows of it rolling across those Kentucky Hills
right down to the bottom lands where the Ohio
brought them the topsoil it had stolen
from the Yankees

we never did find out
what happened
to Uncle Wid's
mules

The Only Thing the Colbys Didn't Touch

was the family graveyard
because there were Colbys buried there

how they got there   nobody knows

I think maybe they snuck in in the night

INFINITE WORLDS

When Jaguars Licked Salt from My Hands

burning jungles
once spread out beneath me
carpets of flame that moved and twisted
following the silver snake of the river
like an evil prophecy

I remember a hot green day
when jaguars licked salt
from my hands
and the shamans turned my body
into a bag of birds

how they pried open my mouth
and stuffed me with parrots
macaws   crested eagles   Fire-eyes
Monjitas   Tinamous   and Cotingas
filled my lungs with feathers
stripped off my skin and replaced it
with a layer of greasy down the color of
rotten mangoes

I remember how my hands became claws
my nails talons
how when I tried to speak
a thousand beaks
came out of my mouth
and my tongue broke off
at the tip

when they were finished
they wrapped me in a blanket of thorns
tied ropes around their ankles
and climbed to the crest
of a great tree

fly   they commanded
throwing me naked and nestless
into air so hot and thick I thought at first
I could swim in it

I flew forever before I hit the ground
flew like a hawk looking for prey
like a vulture looking
for death

now back in these lands
where the leaves turn blood red
and pepper fruits fall to the ground
and everything has a golden
diminishment   as if light itself
is finally being observed to die
I can still feel those birds
trying to beat themselves
out of my skull

and I   almost
take flight again
over that vast jungle
of nightmares and
hallucinations

Before We Were Tattooed

before we were stained and pictured
before our flesh was punctured
before we were inked with all our grievances
we were lovers
blank bodied   kind
featureless as unused paper
none of our secrets
written on our faces
none of our betrayals
inscribed on our foreheads

Solange in Her Youth

In the full of summer when the long days lay before us
and we were young and thought ourselves immortal
we gathered blackberries along the river banks
reaching up to pull down fistfuls of hot sweet fruit
until our hands looked as if they had been dipped in wine

we had no futures on those days
no pasts
only the rapture of floating and gathering
beneath a summer sky hard as an anvil
but you were never content

time stopped for us but it kept flowing for you
sometimes you would climb out of the canoe
and walk barefoot among the thorns
as if steeling yourself against pain
hero of a battle that had not yet taken place
one only you would fight

even then I think you saw another river
stretching out before you black and broad
filled with glowing fish
and the bright discarded feathers of parrots

sometimes you froze among the briars
deaf to our pleas to come back to the boat
froze as if you were listening
to a great, slow rush of water
that would someday bear you away

Suspension

At nine in the evening
when the light was long
and the air still tasted of dust
hot as ashes
we went into the river together
open-mouthed and naked
to consider the proposition
that air was not worth
breathing

that night   our lives
were shadows on the bottom
vanishing in fish
and reeds

think of this the next time
you let water hold you
how love was once
a short summer night
sweet and despairing

Arash's Song

Let me bury my face in your hair
it smells like wheat and roses
Let me bury my body in your flesh
it smells like wild lilies and spring

Am I singing of the Goddess Earth
or my love who sleeps here beside me?

Of both   I sing of both
of the grace of Her brown hills
and the brown curves of your breasts
of your ankles and wrists
and Her saplings that tremble
when the south winds blow

Where Is My Lover

where is my lover?
have you seen him?
I have wandered through the city
calling his name

my friends pity me
they say I've gone mad
at night they sit
in tight circles
lamenting my delusions
       she loves a phantom
       they say
       she loves no one

ah
but they've never lain beside you
in the tall grass
where the deer come down
to lick the summer salt
they've never felt
your lips move
like wings
across the breasts
of the hills

Why Have You Left Me

why have you left me
like this
alone and afraid?

when I hear another man's voice
I turn
thinking
He's come back!
but I only see strangers
with faces
like shovels

I am waiting for my lover
not for you
your hearts are like jars full of bolts
but my lover has a voice smooth as winter honey

The Green River

the green river washes
between my legs
cold as winter mint
if I were clean
I would run with it
down the purple gullied hills
to the ocean

I have been waiting
too long for your love
now when I see
the red-tipped oak leaves
I think of falling things
long wet seasons
dead grass

another year
without you

Our Lady of Dengue

When I die   I will be a blade inside you
your head will fall before me like a cut peony
and your heart will sit in my hand like a small bird
pulsing   trapped   unable to fly.

listen   hear the hiss of my descent
hear this wind of my torment   this snake of steel

Vertigo

a cama vira / the bed turns over
o quarto vira /
the room turns over

look how quickly
we can fall
into darkness

Infinite Worlds

*The limitless content of our universe might be only
one instance of a large (and possibly infinite) number
of other universes.*

—Astronomer Seth Shostak,
Director of the Center for SETI Research

When you lift your fork an infinite number of yous
all lift their forks at the same instant   and an infinite number
are missing their mouths   and an infinite number are choking
on the tines   and an infinite number are being struck by meteors
and vaporized and an infinite number are being trampled by
cattle or time-traveling mammoths or naked strippers
who look like Martha Washington   and an infinite number
of the strippers are sprouting purple wings just as Christ
is coming back in the form of an infinite number of small green aliens
who are explaining they are a poetry collective
that specializes in holographs
and apologizing for the cultural disruption their guy-on-the-cross
experiment made   and that fork keeps rising and rising and destroying
everything in its path as you commit suicide an infinite number
of times   and give birth to an infinite number of babies who drown
in an infinite number of great rivers 150 miles wide which suddenly
appear out of nowhere carrying schools of voracious piranhas
who devour an infinite number of yous forks
before they turn into infinite numbers of gold, rats
hairpins and hockey sticks

because

when there are an infinite number of worlds anything can
happen   and will an infinite number of times   which is why
the idea of infinity   like all things that have no limits
is impossible to grasp even in your own kitchen over a plate
of fried potatoes with a red-handled stainless steel
fork

Pile of Rocks

mounds of back sand smooth as tongues
wrap around our feet like lips
behind a curtain of glittering ash
the waves weave and unweave
threads of molten glass

this morning
six fishermen brought up a monster in their nets
something twisted and so old it had no name

look at those rocks we call a hill

an old man is fighting his way out of the cracks
smeared with egret tailings
just below him   half-buried children
are trying to claw their way through a pile of skulls

let us command those rocks
to be rocks   only rocks

let's pretend this is really a beach

The Citizens of Pompeii Shelter in Place

an orange salt cake in the middle of a green acid pond
salt rafts   salt foam   the salty sting of vog

Lava Creek   Huckleberry Ridge
Yellowstone Lake
(Please don't feed the bears)

Kasbek   Lokbatan   Daht-Nawar
"a nice hotel with a view of the Taal volcano"

the sky burns
the earth shifts
liquid rocks flow to the sea

and the fourth angel poured out his vial upon the sun
And every island fled away, and the mountains were not found

The Last Act

the dancers take the stage
masked as macaws, eagles, elephants
black swans
one is a large ball of army ants
one an entire jungle

by the last act
they have all been done to death

as the last tiger falls to the floorboards
the audience realizes
it has just witnessed real murder

outside the theater
everything is being erased
glass towers
boulders, tumblers of wine
fine cheeses, toy sailboats
children playing hopscotch

the prairie grasses
form a cathedral
over the last living locust
from the west
comes a rumble of thunder and buffalo

Raptor

fever circles
radiant and graceful as an eagle
rising into the air
with something clutched in its claws

great journeys always begin this way
first flat light   silence
weight with no substance
then suspicion
certainty
fear   flight

Land of Smoke

fever makes its own world
an apple a pony
something that tastes like dirt and sugar
grave stones *cachaça*

the flesh is nothing
a visitor
a vehicle
a tourist without a map
lost in a land of smoke
sharp stones
and terror

105 Degrees and Rising

it lifts me from my bed
in an ascending spiral
whispering my name
over and over
like a disappointed lover

gripping me in its claws
gagging me with its shadow
until my flesh turns to iron and the world
becomes a pane of glass
so brittle I can break it
with my tongue

In This Burning World

on the long road down the hill
the cobblestones tip us like drunken sailors
under a sky smeared with volcanic dust

at the bottom lies a sea
clear and pale as the skin
beneath our arms

in this burning world
where we can never stop to rest
you reach out and brush
the tips of my fingers

our parched skin flakes off
in tiny bits and floats up toward the sun
riding the great cone-shaped thermals
of this slowly turning planet

we are two birds
gliding through an empty sky
lost   uncertain
filled with unreasonable joy

Painted Tigers

overhead a great snake of stars
is coiling and uncoiling like boiling water
while beneath the river   the ghost trees
sleep like abandoned dogs

when you come here blind and mute
to dream beside this forgotten shore
when your eyes are too heavy with remorse
to see inward your lips too dry with lies
to form words and your brain filled with
everything you have abandoned
the painted tigers will stalk you on soft pads
admiring the vulnerability of your neck
the tenderness of your flesh
marveling at the way you walk along these paths
never looking back
as if the jungle were yours
as if an animal without teeth or claws
could survive in this place where even the smallest
insect is death's messenger

how gently they will put their muzzles to your mouth
how quickly suck out your breath
how ecstatically breathe in your dreams
the last thing you will feel
will be the softness of their fur
the quick joy of their teeth

Ghost Jaguars

by day   you told us   the dead crouch in the jungle
arms wrapped around their knees
heads down   blind
living in a great blueness
that expands to the horizon
like an infinite ocean

at night they rise
and hunt ghost jaguars
drink the black drink
fuck the trees

we threw your *yopo* seeds on the ground
and trampled them
begged you to come back to us
but you had already eaten your gods
gone hunting with the dead
seen the sun rise and gone blind

Army Ants

a black river
flowed down our walls
smeared the floor under our cots
ate everything scorpions snakes
mice   termites

they would have eaten us too
if we had not fled

later we stumbled on them
sleeping in the jungle
in a great humming ball
their bodies linked into corridors
their dead made into bridges
their pale queen at the center
bloated and quivering

Troops of Brightly Colored Monkeys

troops of brightly colored monkeys
hang from the branches of the Chicona trees

under the Barrigona palms
orange fishing spiders
with venom more toxic than cobras
are weaving gigantic snares
that billow like silver sails

why these strange creatures?
why this fevered nightmare?

the jungle says *eu sou grande* / I am vast
você é pouco / you are nothing
no one is going to save you
no one is going to helicopter you out of here

Castoffs

I no longer care what I leave behind
I kick off my shoes   my feet   my flesh

when I lift up this book
the type falls off the page
when I tilt my head
the sun falls out of the sky

I Went into the Jungle Seeking Hallucinations

I drank nothing   ate nothing
yet the fevers
made me prophetic

what is there to tell?

before the sun went out
and the giant monkey frogs
began to trill
I spoke in tongues
and danced with a dozen empty coke bottles
that whirled around my head
like auras of burnt sugar

as the stars uncoiled above me
my body became transparent
I held my own heart in my hand
and as it drummed
I tasted the future

after that? I can't remember much
I dimly recall, the way you recall a waking dream,
that for hours I chewed on butterflies

once I panicked, ripped a hole in the air, and saw
ecstatic monsters copulating swans
birds with human faces
that wept blood

for 40 years I breathed in nothing but ashes
nursed a snake at my breast
blinded myself with two broaches like Oedipus
and ate my own lips

and the worlds I saw
oh those worlds of the future
you do not want to know
what they look like

Are Animals Immortal?

go away
stop reading this
it won't do you any good
Os animais têm alma?
Nemésio asks
do animals have souls?

who the fuck cares?

the question is:
do you have one?
do I?
and no one knows

no one

all the tales of life after death
are made up
no one has come back
ever   we won't see
the people we loved again
ever
try facing that at four
in the morning

You see
I warned you
this is doing you no good
turn on the television
play a computer game
get laid

Se têm
if they have souls

são imortais, não são?
animals are immortal, right?

if they have souls

if

I'm giving you
one last chance
stop reading now
never think of this again
it doesn't help me or you
or anyone

it's darkness it's silence
it's nothing

this is not a poem
do not mistake it for one

My Mother Comes Floating By

my mother comes floating by
with her skirts spread like Ophelia
again she is threatening to commit suicide
again she won't go through with it

I bow to my mother
who taught me compassion
because she could not feel it
my mother
who could brag about me
but never bring herself to love me

I bow to my mother
who taught me how anger
can ruin the small things in life
how it can make you lonely
how it can separate you from love

I want to go to her   rescue her
bring her back to shore
comfort her
but she cannot be comforted

now that she is dead
I can only speak to her soul

I bow to my mother
great teacher of compassion
my mother
whom the river is taking
toward all the terrors she created

I bless her
I thank her
I watch her float away

PART TWO

Selected Poems 1974–2014

A THREATENING LETTER
TO SHAKESPEARE
(1974 – 1987)

Juliet

I was a green girl
fourteen and fresh
my breasts curled
so tight in my chest
that they ached
time pulled through
my body like sap
and I thought love
grew everywhere
like milkweed

Romeo was a human
swagger
we drove over the state
line near the end
of spring
and were married by
a judge in stripped
pajamas
who loaned us a
cigar band
for a ring

I said
look how the dogwood is
in bloom
like the lips of small children
in the naked woods
and Romeo said
let's stop
for a cheeseburger

I said
when I see a river

I imagine a mouth
at the end
that could swallow us
both

I said
this is the beginning
of a great adventure
I said
I have escaped
into love
and I'll never be
unhappy again

but there was wax
to take off the kitchen floor
and diapers to wash
and Romeo snored
and I found that love
grows around the heart
like the bark on a
tree
and we had three
children
and nobody died
and you can wait forever
for the balcony scene

Ophelia

1.

Ophelia
they say you floated
sang and floated
picking flowers
lilies their sexual cups
pointed pollinated stigma
the soft flesh of violets
you picked their veins
they said
you floated and sang
and your skirts
your heavy wet skirts
dragged you down

true
I believe it
my own skirts
so many things
so wet and heavy
unbearable at last
have dragged me down

I sang too
I floated
drifted through being
a young lady
with crossed legs
like crossed bones
a pirate without a skull
drifted too through being a wife
ironed, cooked,
scrubbed out tubs

sang they said
sang and floated
always drowning
singing floating
Ophelia
even naked I
am still trapped in your
heavy wet skirts

2.

No
no Ophelia no
they said you didn't notice the stream
they claimed you were crazy
said you didn't notice the
slow suction
(homes can be whirlpools
every day women are sucked down
their own drains
women awash
treading water
pulled under
over and over
over and over
damn the waste!
damn the undertow!)

Ophelia
they lied about you
you noticed all right
only you refused to swim
you wanted to lie
looking at the leaves
you preferred to pull apart
the petals of crab apples

petal by petal
piece by piece
like flakes of glass
fish food Ophelia
you and the flowers
food for the fishes

you preferred that second of being buoyed
that long compulsion
of sustained balance
only a second above the surface
you went down
(I think)
by choice

after all
what was there for you
back at the castle
your brother
your father
and what's his name?

Hamlet

Desdemona

I carry this house
on my back
like a turtle
at night I dream
it has grown
under my skin
and grafted itself
to my bones

the white rooms
weigh me down
like sinkers

I know out there
somewhere
the rest of you
are making love

when I wake
in the morning
beside me in bed
my husband's
heavy body
milks away
my breath

Cleopatra

my body
she says
was roses once
and reeds from the Nile
my blood was resin wine
and my hair a skein
of black silk

I wanted to be
a pyramid once
standing alone in the desert
I wanted to be a fertile river
I wanted to be the moon

I wanted to stay
ten years old
forever
sink my roots in the mud
become a papyrus
make a scroll of myself
and never marry

when I was a girl
I was a hieroglyph
but now I'm a whore
to Caesar

now I dance topless
in a leopard-skin
G string
Queen of the Nile
Priestess of Isis
twirling tassels
with silicone breasts

bigger than beach balls

never having any power
of my own
I've learned to seduce it

generals
emperors
businessmen
politicians
and professors
stand in line
to power my ass

I wanted to be
a pyramid once
I wanted to be
the moon

now at night
sometimes
I feel
death
crawling towards me
on its belly

Lady Macbeth

I have seen her at the Corporation
charm classes leaning how to be
the perfect Company Wife

she relocates every three years
with no complaint
serving the same dry martini
from Denver to Dallas

picking the right mate is important
for a Scottish nobleman
on his way up

the castle is drafty
she has nothing to do
in the afternoons she drinks
and walks the battlements

"why don't you try to get ahead?"
she nags her husband at night
when he's trying to go to sleep
"why don't you try to be somebody for a change?"

"the king in charge
is no smarter than you
why he's not even really
executive material."

"play golf with the old man
take him falconing on the moor
invite him back to dinner
and when his back's turned
we'll kill him with a butter knife."

these helpless women
are the most dangerous

"someday," she tells her husband
sucking the pimento out of an olive,
"someday *I* will be Queen."

at night she walks in her sleep
blood on her lips
blood on her hands
her husband takes up more than half the bed

"we're dividing one life"
she mutters
"we're dividing one life
and I want *all* of it."

Split Ends
(1974)

POEMS FROM THE EARLY YEARS OF
SECOND WAVE FEMINISM

What Do You Say When a Man Tells You, You Have the Softest Skin

do you say
it's progesterone, progesterone makes it soft?
when he says
you have big brown eyes
do you say
of course
I'm nearsighted?

my body grew in rings
like a tree trunk
at the center I'm always 10
at the center I'm always wearing
pink plastic glasses
braces
wire wrapped around my head
a mouth full of rubber bands
I have buck teeth I can spit through
corrective shoes
pimples
no legs
no butt
no breasts

one day my mother buys me falsies
overnight I grow from 28AA to 36D
I look down and notice I can't see my feet
I feel like a forklift
I imagine they are realies

in gym the girls steal my bra
and throw it in the pool
my rubber breasts float away
like humpbacked whales

I dive for them
over and over
I dive for my breasts
and come up flat

what do you say when a man tells you
you're beautiful?
do you tell him
"I'm still fishing
I'm still fishing for my body

MLA

early in the morning
the weight of dreams
tears apart the earth
sleep cracks
my bed buckles under me
and I see
the Women's Contingent
from Afkarstan
an imaginary Soviet Republic
and they invite me to come with them to teach

Semyion Semyionovitch
is the Head
(bald)
of the University of Afkarstan
and is known in academic circles
for his *Definitive Work On The Comma.*
I walk into his office
(it reminds me somehow
of the MLA Convention in Chicago
hotel room interviews for non-existent jobs
and in each room and man sitting on the edge of the bed
saying
you look too young to have a doctorate
saying
what about your husband?
will he come with you?
what about your husband, please?
in Spanish, French, Russian
please
explain.
do you intend to have children?
are you happily married?
what about your husband?

would leave him to find work?
really leave him?
what about your husband?
and, by the way,
what did you say
you could teach?)

Anyway
back to the dream
and Semyion Semyionovitch
(from Afkarstan) who
suddenly grabs his couch
and spreads its legs
the couch becomes a trampoline
and he does flips
saying
I'm Head of the University
he bounces up and down in front of me
a bald ball
being very impressive
knee-drops, forward rolls
I am, he says,
Head of the Department
We are looking for a woman
(he pulls me down next to him on the trampoline)
we are looking for a women, he tells me,
I'm Head of the Department, he says
I could get you the job
I'm the Head
(he tries to French kiss me
I fight trying to say
Afkarstan is the same as here
another America
why should I leave now?)
we are looking for a woman, he goes on,
at present we only have 2.6
and the .6 women only has one leg

she has been teaching Freshman Composition
for the last 300 years
for 36 cents per hr.
I could get you a better deal than that
he promises, flipping over on top of me.

this time
instead of his tongue
he sticks
his whole head in my mouth
skull and all
I'm Head of the Department, he reminds me from inside
the voice is a little muffled
like from inside an oil drum
I can feel his neck between my lips
gagging me
I want to bite through it
snap his spine
like a Praying Mantis
I want to lay eggs all up and down his body

someday soon, I warn him,
someday soon
my daughters will eat you.

In Indiana

In Indiana
the corn comes up sharp
green
like shards of glass
broken glass
broken fields

this spring the whole country is
splintered

my sister walks beside me
grow up strong I tell her
lift weights
push up
have strong arms
strong legs
hands that can crush things

don't be like me
another weak woman
fingers like lace
a paper doll

my sister does not hear me
already she is dancing
barefoot in the corn
her feet turn the earth
her body is straight
hard as a cob
her breasts are small
unripe kernels
her feet turn the earth
my sister is dancing
her feet turn the earth
like the blades of a plow

One Night Stand
(1976)

One Night Stand

you were a four-star fuck
you went on and on
like meditation
or ballet
executing impossible leaps
adopting positions
previously attempted
only by pretzels

at the end
I had
an urge
to rise up clapping
and cry
"Encore!"

but I had
accidentally
gotten myself
snarled in you
like a fishline

"Excuse me," I mumbled
apologetically, trying to disengage
"I didn't mean
to feel
any tenderness
You see
I suffer from the delusion
that making love
makes love
I hold the insane
conviction
that people

should be more than bags
for each other's phantoms
I imagined
that if I reached
into you
I could pull out
the eagle
that is beating itself
to death
against your ribs
and stroke it
back to sleep."

"Excuse me, please.
I am undergoing
therapy
to cure me of
the habit of caring
and someday I hope
to be
as sane and cold
as any normal
American.

After all
in my lucid interludes
I know
I am only one
of the hundreds
who came down the road
and pulled in briefly
at your
one night stand."

Withdrawal

When we make love
you touch me gently
afterwards you're so hard
I wonder where he lives
that man who comes in me
then leaves so suddenly

Inside
it is the dark of the moon
my belly rises full
from you
polished, waxed like an apple
you fill me with dreams
and visions
and tenderness fragile as breath
I feel you mortal
inside me
and know people
should cling together
precious in their loving
on the long road to death

how fragile you seem then
as if you might snap
against my body like a stick
I put up my arms to
protect you
nourishing, blowing on you
like an ember

and then
suddenly
you turn inside out
and become

well-welded
armor-plated
invulnerable
again
and I break my nails
against your skin
and my heart
against your logic

do you know
why I lie with you?

I lie
only hoping
to meet you
once again
along the road
only hoping
to meet once again
that tender
stranger

Wild Woman

sometimes I imagine I am a frontier woman
lost from my wagon train
wandering
starving
sucking the sweet tips of wild chives
grubbing under the leaves
for beechnuts and acorns
for puff balls gone soft as flesh
stuffed with yellow powder

the snow melts on my tongue
I forget my drawing room
my china cupboard
my ten quilts pieced by hand

at the first thaw
foxes crawl out
leaving warm leaves
old fur
the smell of rotting wood

pulling my hair
I make a snare to catch meat
the wild geese returning
snarl in my net
I coat my skin with their fat
forget my fine complexion
my long white gloves
I am oiled leather now
I shine in the sun
my hair grows long on my head
and under my arms
I spend the night counting the stars
and remembering the husband and children

who, thinking I am dead,
have put up a stone marker

by now
no doubt
I've been carved and dated

they bleed away like ghosts
manless
childless
for the first time
I am not afraid

my feet grow hard as bloodstone
my petticoat falls off
I am naked and tattered
I chew a willow rod to a point
and spear my first trout
I twist my wedding ring into a hook
I survive

at night sometimes I think
I have become the woods
my arms are trees
my fingers twigs
my feet roots
my body disappears like a bad dream

the pools reflect a wild woman
her breath smells of comfrey

I forget the name he gave me
and invent my own

Skin Deep

(1978)

Extractions

I have survived
many operations

at ten they cut
the boy out of me
spit, self-respect
tumorous ambition
Roy Rogers   the Alamo
Bill Vukovich   drained
the crankcase oil from
my veins   the jet
pilot   the spaceman
the wrestler with long
yellow hair
Antigone
the leather child
who whipped the air
like a belt
when she ran

they sewed me up
with silk slips
and French heels
stilts and stockings
and spandex girdles
training bra traction
occupational therapy
white cotton gloves
Miss Gates dancing
school a good follower
one leg always lifted
like a pink flamingo
I learned to wait for
some man to move me

at seventeen in the back
of my boyfriend's Chevrolet
I experienced the removal
of an impacted independence
Artemis   moon bones
the huntress lady of
wild things   my cypress
backbone amputated

after the blood and the silence
the Liebfraumilch   the white
wine   afterwards
in the recovery room
in the bed barred like a pen
I came to   myself
and found she was
gone

marriage was the worst
operation   my heart removed
beating and sticky   a newborn
child   liver replaced with
bridesmaids and blenders
parts of my soul growing
out of control   called
cancerous   mastectomy nodes
of resistance rooted out
grafted like a plum branch
to some alien trunk
Janus-faced
bonsai lady   Demerol
in the veins   masked faces
polite conversation
a clicking of knives   gas
and champagne bubbles
in the blood   the first
tingle of numbness

a severed nerve
small talk   dinner party
anesthesia   spread out
on the table   the piece
de resistance   the
perfect hostess

Separate Beds

in the living room
you have made
a nest of dry leaves
and bones
like a wolf
you have piled
freshly killed things
around you
rabbit skins
and dead dreams
and cushions stuffed
with my hair

in New York
your body
curled into mine
like black paper
stuck to me
like a silhouette
our bones
were like a cheese grater
and our eyes
were hot yellow stones

in New York
when we were young
and poor
and hungry
and sick
we held each other

now two doors
cut our love
in half

the taxidermist has
stuffed our lives
we keep them
in separate boxes

back in our bed
I sleep with pennies
on my eyes   and even the cat
finds my body
too cold to touch

Lot's Wife

my bones are the stones
of the earth
bleach and break
crack and bend
they will all blend again
flesh to loam

I am bitter to the tongue
I have come down a narrow trail
bearing heavy burdens
I have carried in the seasons on a stick
borne the change of winter worn to spring

my lifetime has carved
a pass through these mountains
I have been a dry creek cutting a canyon
an olive tree rooted in stone

2.

those who turn
turn to salt
those who stop in the snow
freeze in the snow
those who stop in time
stick in time
like flies

love webbed me to this world
I was spun from my own wool
loomed on my own loom
I made a clay jar of my life
and kilned it closed

now at last I drop it
carelessly along the way

The Woman in the Moon

my great-grandmother
married at sixteen
a blue-eyed Irish woodworker
who promised to build her
a life out of apple wood
and cherry
instead he gave her
thirteen children
drank up the rent
and died of blood poisoning
while building a carriage
shaped like a shoe

for forty years
she lived alone
dressed in black
like a retired witch
in a house full of chests
and chairs and wooden clocks
waiting for him
to come home again

when she was eighty
and I was four
we met
her skin was so thin
by then that you could
see her veins like grain
she kept her teeth
in a glass of water
and her heart in a rosewood
box by the door

there is a woman in the moon
my great-grandmother told me
who carries a bundle of sticks
on her back

each month she swells
each month she declines
like many women
she has married a burden
and must bear it forever
across the sky

life bends us, she told me
my own life was scrap wood
my own life was sorrow
thick as a board

tell all your daughters
to build something better
burn kindling
not carry
keep one eye on the sky

On the Dark Side of the Moon

on the dark side of the moon
a golden egg lay in a crater
shaped like the pause
between two breaths
beat like a heart
a hummingbird hidden
in the palm of my hand

I swallowed it whole
felt it roll inside me
unsteady as a half-loaded ship
riding an invisible tide

on the seventh wave the egg
penetrated my womb
and I became pregnant with space
immaculate and alien
the whites of my eyes gold
my lips my hands gold
foil skin beaten out across my cheeks
gold swelling from my hips
I was the expanding universe
I gave birth to marvelous creatures

one spoke in colors instead of words
another was covered with small dry twigs
the third lay storms to rest
the fourth made orchards grow
where bones had been

the fifth was a blue messiah
she fed the world at her breast
she trimmed the dead leaves from plants
with the cutting edge of her desire

her fingers were like a field of green wheat
she drove souls before her like warm rain

the sixth came to destroy all impediments
he levelled the hills and burnished
the earth to a ball
there was glass in my bread
I gave birth to the seventh while lying
on a mirror

the egg inside me cracked
I rose and created a new creation
I invented animals
I organized the clouds
I swung the moon around
in a pause between two breaths

this is a true story
I know
I dreamed it

The Dear Dance of Eros
(1987)

We Made Love Until I Couldn't

remember my name
out on the borders of
morning where everything was snow
white hot like grits
and cream

the smell of your salt was on
my back and there were long
tunnels where buses became beasts
from the Pleistocene   I saw
pterodactyl wings sprout
from your fingers felt
the rush of your breath fanning my
neck   how naked it all was   all those tiny
blond hairs on my spine hanging like
a necklace down your chest then
the walls collapsed and the whole room fell
down my throat like a deck of cards

you curled back
my head and held my mouth
open like I was
a rattlesnake
and we began all over
again
god save us I thought this is
madness

but you were man
sweet and not
to be resisted
and my tongue became a song
bird and I wanted to walk
through your body

and come out the other
side in that land
where lovers live in each other
forever
like fish

Love and Other Major Disasters

passion is like anthrax
or the bubonic plague
I kiss the open palm of your hand
and think
cicatrice, wound, stigmata
(nothing can cut me away from you
alive)

passion is like the earthquake
that topples the house
piles of plaster
a kettle incongruous on a broken stove
and somewhere the hiss of leaking gas
(you see   I would destroy everything
for you)

passion is like the typhoon
that breaks off the palm trees
swamps the island
batters the fish against the beach

passion feeds on disaster
like flies feed on meat
down deep
in the cone of the volcano
in the burning house
in the head-on collision
the place where the road is always littered
with fresh glass

(a siren passes by
underneath our window
with five thin bones
you pull down the shade)

Snow

Cocaine's for horses and not for men
Doctor says it'll kill you but don't know when
—Dick Jordan "Cocaine Blues"

you joined the expedition
to the pole
pulled out on your sled
leaving me behind

you disappeared
over the rim
of the great white horizon
of the world
on iced runners
like a spot of ink
falling off the page

the first blizzard
numbed your nose
the second your gums
the third your throat, your lungs,
your hands, your heart
finally your soul crystallized like a geode
and you were drifted in
for a long winter
and your days were all darkness
and your nights were anesthetic
cold and deep

you said you felt no pain
you said you had never done anything
wrong

you said you were always happy
high on the ice
at the top of the world

but you don't walk the same
and you don't talk the same
and your body is as blue as a jazz note
and when you open an envelope
your hands shake
and your words stumble out of your mouth
like crippled birds

and as for love, dear,
I think you fed it
to your dogs

Clearing the Land

take a snake
to your bed dear
gray blue
flat-headed thing
so grateful
to curl between
your breasts
animal gratitude
is what we all want

your lips are
stained with wine
and there is a red
tinge to your teeth

up on the mountain
the rest of us are dancing
with grape leaves in our hair
one woman has gone mad
she lies on the ground
her white wool robe
pulled over her face
keening in the spring
in her hands
there is something
torn in half

she chants that
no one loves her
and that someone
will have to pay

we put her out like a fire
this is no maidens' ring
we are all veterans
of some hunt or other

we are decorated with
our scars
by nightfall
we will have cleared this land
of everything alive
and begun to feast
upon each other

Cytherea

Quivering fins
ridged like rakes
a sliding, gill-chambered tongue—
the inside of her mouth
is yellow and blue
barracuda silver
sweet as red mullet
stripped with black and green
with peacock flounder teeth
pink and sharp and quick

Cytherea is angry
that we have poisoned her oceans
at night she climbs the waves
straddles the white foam
and calls to her whales
"are you catfood yet?"
she howls
"have they made you all
into lipstick and soup?"

She is unforgiving
and methodical
when a dolphin gets tangled
in a tuna net
she grieves
when a single cell of green algae dies
she knows it

She has picked the brains
of all the philosophers who ever drowned
looking for the causes of human folly
she has mastered the concept of original sin
and thinks there may be something to it

she is acquainted with the theory of eternal forms
which holds that if the oceans of earth die
the idea of oceans will persist unchanged
in some godly sphere of boredom and perfection
but the only oceans Cytherea cares about
are these
bitter and dirty
salty and dying
these small mortal oceans
it makes her weep to see them

the rusting barrels of nuclear waste
drive Cytherea to distraction
she plots revenge
with the cunning of a shark—she
who was so peaceful
that the Phoenician sailors
wrote odes to her patience
calling her dove soft
smoother than their wives
purple skinned and lovely
as the harbor of Tyre
when the shellfish blossom
oh lovely sea goddess
they wrote,
we move across your belly
like bridegrooms
singing your praises

Now she sits in a dark cave
consorting with morays
sipping poison drinks
concocted from the venom
of Australian stone fish
counting the tankers
that rumble overhead
breathing the oil-fouled water

assimilating the toxins
through her seaweed soft skin
she is not pleased
she is not amused

Cytherea is planning something
down there
something she tells only
to the spiny batfish
and sea dragons
perhaps she has decided
to call back the oxygen
and leave us gasping
perhaps she has decided
to melt her ice caps
rise and take back all the cities
that ever emptied sewage
down her throat
perhaps she has decided to show us
a mercy we don't deserve—
but don't count on it

Cytherea
the flowers we throw to you
come back oil-soaked
and dying
We stand on your beaches
calling you up
but you no longer appear
at our feet you scatter
pieces of styrofoam cups
tin cans, beer bottles, hunks of insulation,
stinking fish and dead birds
and sometimes a jellyfish
pulsing and dying
like a punctured soap bubble
like a human heart
gone bad.

Bag Lady

I knew a long time ago
that you were going down
I dreamed of lifeboats
and water in the mouth
the first time I saw you

in the opening scene
you are sitting in front of your mirror
looking at the watermarks on the glass
wedding bows all broken
seven years without a birth
you can see at a glance
the bad times are beginning

> *how dry my skin is*
> *there are liver spots on my face*
> *my great great great grandmother*
> *was burned for a witch*
> *I am feeding the cat fresh cream*
> *and this act I know*
> *will testify against me*

in the next scene you are taking a needle
out of a drawer
but you can no longer see the eye
the threads of your life
have become the filaments of a phantom
behind you the children
are fighting with knives

> *lint lies in the corners*
> *the bathtub is yellow*
> *I do not move the plants*
> *when I dust them*

to tell the truth
I no longer dust
this act I know
will testify against me

in the third scene
you are looking at the side of the bed
where your husband once slept
you are looking at your bankbook
at your children's empty shoes

I'm a widow lady and I live alone
at night I put on the Victrola
and play New Orleans jazz
ten years ago
the car swerved into a bread truck
and I was crippled
but I go on dancing just the same
I'm a widow lady who wears red
instead of black
this act I know
will testify against me

when you were young
there were no roads
or trucks
only wagons and mud paths
lacing the countryside
mules and windmills
and the clean white waste
of winter snow

now in the last scene
out on Sycamore Street
you mumble to the traffic
an ill-natured old crone
with paper bags full of trash

dragging a roll of asphalt roofing behind you
like a queen's train
and cursing a man dead
these twenty years

> *oh you had affairs damn you*
> *I knew you did*
> *but I kept my mouth shut*
> *because of the children*
> *may they rot in hell*
> *for never calling*
> *a mother, what's a mother?*
> *a bag stuffed with junk*
> *and fifteen cents for a bottle*
> *I spent my whole life picking up*
> *after other people*
> *and then you had to go and die*
> *damn your eyes*
> *heart attack*
> *I knew you had affairs*
> *when we were first married you called me*
> *your darling baby girl*
> *now I got to catch the number 17 bus*
> *Sam Sam why don't you love me like*
> *you used to*
> *Tommy, Alice, Andy look both*
> *ways before you cross*
> *the ashes to ashes and*
> *dust to I just can*
> *'t take it any mo*
> *re   these words*
> *you all   have testified*
> *against me*

Betony

by the time
we came across the gap
through the Cumberlands
it was late spring
and I was driving the wagon alone
my husband was buried
under a buckeye tree
five days back
two of the children
had milk fever
and the third lay
sick at my breast

it was a violent
blue-green Kentucky spring
mushrooms raised their humps
over every log
and the waters were roiled
with strange fish

the first year we ate
acorns and nearly starved

you need a husband
the neighbors said

the second year
the cabin burned
and I covered my children
with leaves
and nested down with them
like a squirrel

you can't live without a man

my neighbors told me

the third year
we ate our own corn
at our own table
the forest around us was blessed
we killed nothing
the earth opened up to our seeds
the sun and the rain
came in perfect order
and the squashes in the garden
swelled like pregnant women

I took coltsfoot and barberry
and conceived a fourth child
she was born with a tiny ring
of blood around her wrist
and eyes were as soft
as new bark
when she walked
wildflowers grew in her footprints
her bones were fine and hollow
she flew over her sisters
like a jackdaw

I called her Betony
and the neighbors said
I was mad

she will grow sweet to the taste
I told them
she will cure all wounds
she will be Betony
the spiked plant
the wood mint
the woman alone
who sanctifies

Grand Jetée

some rhythms must remain unbroken

like a dancer in an
arabesque
some women cannot carry
a child
in their arms

some come to salvation
drawn by the hands of small children

some can only make their leaps

alone

Breaking the Fever
(2006)

Breaking the Fever

When I was young
fevers were attacked
the grown-ups would rub you
with alcohol
wrap you in wet sheets
refuse you blankets
fan you, feed you aspirin
plunge your wrists in cold water

they knew fever had to be fought
because it let children see
forbidden things
At 105 I would start to hear voices
soft and lulling
at 106 the faces would appear
swimming around me

stretching out their hands
they would gesture to me
to join them
I was always very happy then
floating out on the warm brink
of the world

the fever children
would sing in high voices
liquid like silver bells
come with us
they would say
come play, Mary
and they would show me
maple trees turning red and gold
long aisles of sunlight
and woods that glowed and trembled

My body would start to come apart
very gently like milkweed fluff
and I would begin
to rise up toward their
hands
but always at the last moment
the dark circles
of the grown-ups' faces
would force me back down
and their fear would pin my chest
to the mattress
like black crystal paper weights

They would force more aspirin on me
more ice and alcohol rubs
more wet sheets
and if that didn't work
they would lift my naked body
and plunge it into a tub of cold water
ignoring my screams

Come back
they would plead
come back
come back
and my fever would buckle
and snap like the spine
of a beautiful snake
crushed under a boot

Then the fever children
would abandon me
and I would be left in a world
of ordinary things:
light bulbs
used Kleenex

hissing radiators
thermometers

I would see my mother's pale
terrified face
and my stuffed animals
and my brother's crib
and my precious fever would lie
broken in a thousand bits
with no way to put it back together
and I could never explain
how kind it had been
and how foolish we were to fear it

First Grade

Miss Logston
said we should
make our
O's
like balloons
she took our
hands in hers
and crushed
our knuckles
like nuts
she made us
draw circles
for hours
round & round
like vultures
circling a
dead donkey

Miss Logston
smelled of
violets
she stuffed
our mouths
with tissue
taped them shut
grabbed us
by the hair
and shook us
senseless

she said
if we talked
out in class
or chewed

gum
or wet our
pants
we would go
to a dark place
where flies
without wings
would crawl over
our open eyes
forever

she
said
we were her
best class
in ten years

she said we
showed
promise

Methodist Grandmother Said

My Methodist
grandmother said
dancing
was adultery
set to music

how right she was

in that sweet sway
breast to breast and
leg to leg
sin comes into its own

if you have never
waltzed
you cannot imagine
the sheer voluptuousness
of it
the light touch
palm to palm
wool and silk
mixed below the waist
your partner's warm breath
on your neck
coming quicker
and quicker
the strength of the man
the yielding of the woman
so incorrect
so atavistic
so unspeakably sweet

he moves toward you
you back away

he pursues you
and with the faintest
pressure
you encourage him
and watch the blood
rush to his face

not a word is spoken
no one sees this
although it's done in public
in full sight of everyone

you touch
and retreat
meet
and touch again
in time to the music
saying yes
no   yes
no   yes
no
yes

you dance
without thinking of your body
in that gentle
rhythmic
careless
almost copulation

one   two   three
one
two   three

the longest
foreplay
in the western
world

L. Tells All

I wanted a man
but they were in
short supply
so when this big white
swan followed me home
and announced
"I Am Zeus, Lord of All Creation,"
I crooked my finger at him
and said
"come here, Bird Boy,
let's give it a try."

at first
I have to admit
it was fun
his soft breast
the excited squawk
the way he beat his wings
frantically
like an umpire gone bad
but basically
it was an act of
desperation

we had nothing in common
his feathers made me sneeze
I was afraid to fly
he was married
(of course
they all are)
and we even had religious differences

what can I say?

and then there were his other
women
Io, Europa, Semele
(not to mention the
sluttish little pens he picked up
in the park)

we started to have
terrible fights
I called him an overstuffed
pillow and threw seed
in his face
he threatened to migrate
the usual stuff

by spring
we'd both had enough

one night
while we were sitting
in a Greek restaurant
I told the old cob I'd always
be his friend
but I just couldn't handle
interspecies love

(I lied, of course
the truth was
I'd already started to see
a duck
on the side)

The Breakfast Nook

the vision comes
twice
the object out of context:
first ducks
that look like snorkelers
black silhouettes
against a void
then at breakfast the next morning
the bowl that is no longer a bowl
but a white sound
swirling into
a depression
of unspeakable depth
the tea
a brown ocean
reflecting eight moons
my hand
a crippled starfish
naked, albino
floating up from the depths
holding a fork that has become
a long shining road
that branches at the end
into four paths
that lead nowhere

the spoon explodes
clicking and ringing:
bell sounds
rain on a tin roof
water beaded on flesh
and metal
domes of water

sliding down the side
of a glass
miniature worlds
distorted and luminous
all the senses systematically
deranged

the reflection is pitted
against the void
where no reflection
is possible

death can only be seen upside down
through a pin hole camera

the cat in the mirror
attacks itself

Santa Teresa Calls Him
(But He Does Not Answer)

as she kneels barefoot
in her cell
her longing
for him becomes
so intense she breaks
her vow of silence

putting her lips
to the basin
she blows
his name
into the water
and lets it circle there
a small boat
on a vast
ocean

the flame
of the half-gutted
candle
trembles

slowly
    slowly
        slowly
            his name expands

until her
loneliness
fills
the entire
room

Rumor Had It We Were Eating Dogs

we walked through
towns where
the buildings looked
like blocks of congealed honey
and ate the hearts of animals
broiled on sticks
by old women
who waved away the gnats
with dirty hands

rumor had it
we were eating
dogs
rumor had it
the president
had been assassinated
in his palace
in the capital city
on the other
side of a mountain of
salt

we hoarded rumors like
pennies
why were all the fountains
dry?
why did the lights go out
at ten?
what was the purple fruit
the children sold
that tasted like
gunpowder and
string?

we heard a German
botanist
had seen a man
turn into a
jaguar

we thought he was
hallucinating
we thought he might be
telling the
truth

there were rumors of
peace
rumors of war
rumors that we were
betraying each
other

day after day
the planes
flew
overhead
but none
of them
ever
landed

Memories of My Own Underdevelopment

Mexico: Sunday, October 6, 1968

I went out to buy lady
fingers chopped
off I imagined from the hands
of the great baked
lady
(I was 23 and proud of my wit)

the street smelled like charcoal
and tortillas
there were yellow puddles
narrow bone
colored sidewalks
whole families returning
from church

in the plaza a crowd had gathered

a student in a white
shirt
was making a speech
Su sangre! he kept crying
Their blood! Their blood!

I could not hear
the rest so I imagined
a few cops with
clubs
a few bloody heads
I decided he was
overwrought
the boy lacks rhetorical skills
I thought

maybe if he ate
the baked lady's head
he'd be smarter

(I was 23 and proud of my wit
I had not heard the news)

I walked on
toward the store
thinking of small things
my own small
life
my ladyfingers

suddenly three
trucks
pulled into the
plaza

Su sangre! cried
the student

the metal doors on
the backs of the trucks
  rolled up

inside were
soldiers

who said nothing

they simply
began to
fire

The Mayans Take Back Yucatan

It's the end of an ordinary day:
along the Caribbean coast
black mangrove roots
thick, pulsing and moist
knit the sea to the land;
in the thatched houses near Chetumal
fried beans simmer in iron pots
and the mouths of the children
are slick with hunger

out on the Lagoon of the Seven Colors
near ancient Bacalar
where the Spanish fort
still reeks of conquest and death
moiré patterns suddenly appear out of nowhere
quivering on the purple, violet, pink
mirror of the brackish water
that's the only sign
only those slow circles
moving out from the center of the lagoon
as the earth shudders under them

two thousand miles to the north
the world has ended

the circles on the lagoon
ripple and overlap
lip to lip
like lovers' kisses
crickets pulse
the air cools
an old man throws a net
the sunset is especially beautiful

a few weeks later
they begin to round up the pale ghosts
and repaint the temples
a few rent-a-car agents
are sacrificed
some tourists put to tearing down
the luxury hotels
SUVs with California plates
lie on their sides
along abandoned highways
and empty beer bottles
glitter in the hot sun
the loudest noise at this stage
is the buzzing of flies

in ten years
the cenotes are full of clean water again
the banana-billed toucans
are back
and the fruit bats
have taken over the Hiltons
rare black coral
has reappeared along the coast of Cancun
fat babies doze in the shade

the universe has a new center
a green navel
soft and loose
as a woman's belly after birth
the jungle and the corn
do their old dance together
and butterflies swarm
and multiply

Each morning the Sun God
smacks his lips
comes out of hiding
and climbs back into the sky

When We Were Your Age

we have told you
our youth
was beautiful
we said we danced
naked in the forest
and lay with one another
in the fields

we have shown you pictures
of ourselves
with our arms
around each other
hair plaited
with flowers
tear gas blossoming
behind us
in great white petals
and on every face
a smile
of perfect conviction

we have decorated
our houses with carved gourds
from Peru
stone jars from Greece
and every time
we dust them
we force you
to listen to us tell you that,
when we were your age,
we put everything we owned
in a backpack
and hitched barefoot
across Brazil

slept with cannibals
lived in caves
ate holy herbs
and learned to levitate

we never mention
the nights of dysentery
and raw fear
friends who shot junk
and walked out windows
idiots who refused
to feed their babies
anything but raw broccoli
and acid

our romantic stories
contain no lice
no death
no 18-year-old soldiers
dying in the mud
no speed freaks
in the next room
breaking furniture
and screaming that devils
are coming out of
the kitchen faucets

in these stories
no one ever walks in on her husband
screwing a stranger
on the living room rug
and no one ever has
to be driven
to the psych ward

instead we take to the streets
like packs of jolly elves
the police beat us
but we don't care
we sing
we prevail
we make heroic speeches
about peace and civil rights
we link arms
we dance
we integrate schools
we walk on water
we stop a war
we bring a president
to his knees

the truth is:
we did all that
but we did it bleeding
we did it
afraid

Witness

there were once beasts called elephants
when one could not get food
the others fed her
they were taken for their tusks
which were made into bracelets and piano keys
and their feet, which were made into footstools
the seals were made into hats and coats
the salmon were fished out of the rivers
and eaten
the ostriches were taken for plumes for hats
the giraffes became seat covers

there were once trees
older than our oldest cities
with trunks as thick
as the pillars of temples
near the end people tried to save them
by sitting in the tops
but they were forced down
and the trees became plywood

Swordfish were served in fine homes
on long polished tables
covered with exotic sauces
bones of wild mules were
ground up for glue

Mostly it happened by accident
no one meant to get rid of the frogs
at night they used to sing so loudly
we had to shout over the sound of them
and then one summer they sang softly
and then one summer they stopped singing

the honeybees died of some kind of virus
and then the crops failed
and the fruit trees stopped bearing
and a great silence spread over the fields

small things died
things we hardly noticed:
wild grasses
obscure fish
plants that didn't flower
bacteria
tiny brown birds
a kind of grasshopper that only lived in Africa
a plant that grew high up in a tree in the Amazon
where no human being had ever seen it
a biting gnat that people were glad to see go
clothes moths
a Siberian squirrel
some weeds along the side of the freeway
some silly-looking thing that lived in the sand
that the curlews ate
some tiny green plankton that floated in the sea
that no one knew about

soon only the oldest of us could remember
a time when we woke to the humming of the locusts
when a coyote danced in the sagebrush
a beaver felled a tree
a rhinoceros bathed in the mud
and wild roses bloomed in the ditches beside the roads

on summer evenings
large birds
used to cross the thin golden plate of the sun

in the forests
the whippoorwills sang all night long

Making Important Decisions

he put fist holes
in walls
broke lamps
smashed shades
shattered windows
grabbed up a butcher knife
and slashed a chair
to shreds

was the man dangerous?
I didn't know

he slept with a gun
under his pillow
but I didn't know
he took Ecstasy
and looked at me with
the eyes of a lemur
but I still didn't know

sometimes he talked
in different voices:
the old cowboy
the sad child
the demented woman
who reminded me
of someone
I had once cared for
but whose name
I could no longer
remember

sometimes he told me
he was Christ

or a visitor from another
planet
it seemed oddly reasonable
perhaps he *was* Christ
perhaps all of us
were only
visiting

at night
he listened
to rebirthing tapes
the baby sliding down
the vagina
the thumping of the
mother's heart

You are making important
decisions
the voice on the tape
warned
decisions
that will affect
the rest of your life

but I paid no
attention

I was making
no decisions
there with Christ
in my bed
with the alien beside me
with the gun
under the pillow
six inches from
my
head

Lynchburg

you are not
walking through this field
of yellow flowers

you are not here
you have never been here
you are making yourself from
moment to moment

the blackberry brambles
are making themselves
the cars on Route 29
are making themselves
the sanctuary oaks are making
themselves

nothing is where you left it
it was never there
your shoes are not where you left them
your lovers are not where you left them
even your heart is not where you left it
a moment ago

the cannonballs buried in the forest
under the alders and buckeye trees
are not the same cannonballs
that General Hunter's boys fired
at General Early's boys
each ball
keeps making itself
and every time it makes itself
something is changed
and something is lost

the Confederate boys made themselves
into grass
and the Yankee boys made themselves
into gravel roads
they made themselves into cold fronts
coming in from the north
and tornadoes
sweeping across from the west
and hurricanes blowing in
from the Gulf
and sycamores
and pines
and red dirt

and the widows of the boys
made themselves
into wild onions
plantain
and dandelions
stumps of old trees
fields of hay
and red gashes in the grass where
the new bypass
is coming through
into kudzu
and clover
white rocks
brick buildings
and small windows
with neat wooden frames
libraries
and spent hunting shells
black cows loose on the road
and they're still remaking themselves
moment by moment
into empty beer cans
and girls with long hair

and trucks carrying packages
and propane

the mules that hauled the cannons
made themselves into creeks
and hot asphalt
and the horses the officers rode
made themselves into railroads
and dogs
churches
and broken plumbing
and rust
and they keep on remaking themselves
like the ragweed
and wild roses
that line the ditches
along Coldwell Road

the birds are
relearning their songs
from moment to moment
the kernels of corn
the leaves of the tobacco plants
the mud in the river
have no duration

on that June day in 1864
when the ones in gray rode in on the train
from Charlottesville
and the ones in blue walked over the rise
everything around them
was dying and being reborn

so the boys
took aim
and made
each other

into deer ticks
and mice
the sweet center
of common white clover
dust on windows
in the stables where
the wealthy girls keep
their horses
distant thunder
crows
and a woman in a green T-shirt
bending down
to pick an armful
of flowers

Samba

Samba
samba
it's always
been
samba

the ferns
in the window
samba
toward the light

the squash
blossoms in the
garden
samba open
and the cucumber
vines samba
up the wall

in the high grass
the crickets
are singing
samba
and the quail
are in a circle
stamping
their feet

the cabbage moths
samba
and the yellowjackets
samba
and even the snails samba
(very very slowly)

out in the Oort
Cloud
Hale-Bopp is
doing the samba
twitching her
long argon skirts

at the edge
of the universe
at this very
moment
billions of
nameless
galaxies are
sambaing away
from one another
at the speed of
light

back on earth
people samba
to work
and samba home
and their dogs
and cats
samba out
to greet them

lovers
samba
all night long
in samba-happy
beds
and new-born babies
dream of nothing
but samba

even
the dead
samba
into the ground
and samba
back out again
leaving
empty spaces
where the
samba
goes on doing
its own
samba forever

Sugar Zone
(2011)

The Jaguars That Prowl Our Dreams

Up on the Orinoco, Rio Negro, Solimões,
Tocantins, Xingu, Javary
they're drinking the *bebida preta* / black drink
snake vine ayahuasca / yage /   blood of the great anaconda
with the smoke of burning rainforests in their nostrils
and *o gosto de cinzas* / taste of ashes on their tongues

Eles estão comendo   they're eating
purple snails   powdered viper venom
lagartas esmagadas   flowers that dye their lips
the color of blood   singing of cities of blue glass
and the jaguars that prowl our dreams

O que mais / what else   are they seeing?
O que mais / what else   do they know?

they're not saying
they're not telling
they're calling on the ghost tribes instead

ghosts of the *Tupinambá, Tupiniquim, Aimoré*
lost upriver   forever
lost in the burning world

Dreaming of the Bullet-Proof Cars of Maceió

This is the *terra do açúcar e maus sonhos*
the land of sugar and bad dreams
infinite darkness without borders
where birds passing overhead
smell like *biscoitos molhados* / wet crackers
sour milk and the sweat of sex
aqui / here in the night room   doorknobs turn
your hands   mirrors reflect receding galaxies
and the clown who lies on his back beside you
twitching and suffering   is your soul

wake up   *acordar!*   tell me why nothing moves
why starving people lean into their shadows
like flies caught in amber
why the past goes on eating the present
like a rising ocean eats the beach

tell me why they are burning
palm trees on the road to the airport
why the water tastes like ashes
why the windows of the cars are blind

at low tide the children drink cachaça
and call on Iemanjá   fishtailed mother of storms
wake up and tell me why the sand beneath this city
keeps shifting   why all the stores are stocked with
hallucinations   tell me why Solange left
and where she went

Sugar Zone

Sempre me amedrontou   I have always
been afraid   tankers strung out along the horizon
like a necklace of black
seeds   a *idéia de ter um filho*   of the idea
of having a child   let's get drunk
on *cachaça* forget her outstretched
hands her face   the delicate angle of her nose
her children selling candy roses   *cor de pedras*
color of stones amethyst, emerald, diamond
all day the tankers come and go   the mill grinds
barefoot men and women cut
and cut

for a whole week I missed Solange
Por uma semana eu tive saudade
then clarity for three days
limpeza   limpeza
they sleep on the
black and white tiles that wind beneath our feet
steal the food off our plates
We eat behind fences
the ticks drop off the
trees and settle between our cold beer
and cashews   plastic straws blow down the beach
like transparent wands   a *cidade só voltara a existir
depois de 20 de janeiro*   (this city has only existed
since the 20th of January)   for twenty minutes I
stood in the deserted street
    fiquei olhando / looking
for something
            no longer
there

This Is a Poem Creating Itself

Este é um poema criando-se
this is a poem creating itself *em um idioma*
in a language you don't understand

think of it as a dancer
whose face is hidden behind a beaded veil
uma bebida preta   a black drink that
lets you hear jaguars speak
a city seen from 20,000 feet
um barulho / a noise that wakes you *à meia-noite*
tropeçando tropeçando   stumbling through the
darkness   knocking at your door

The Drowning Boys

Down to the Farol do Barra on the Bay of All Saints
out to the raw sugar beaches of Jaguaribe and Itapuã
stomachs empty as charity
bare feet coated with salt and the mud of melted hills
Eles estão chegando   here they come
the drowning boys / *as moleques da rua*
from Susuranna, Favela de Alagados,
Maciel / Pelourinho   coming in packs
like dancing saints   their faces bright as the mirror
Iemanjá holds when she walks on the waves

as crianças sem esperança   the boys without hope

how gently they will touch our wrists
as they unstrap our watches
how carefully they will turn us over
as they empty our pockets & push us under

these children who don't fear death
children who   in another life
we might have loved

Conquistadors

Until the fall of the first rains
we possess nothing but hope
the streets of this lost city
are tracks of black salt
spilled on a table
wounded dancers weaving drunkenly
past sleeping dogs

at night we dream of high cliffs
studded with crystals
tunnels that lead to palms
and water

the heat is a long hiss
a desert of bones
a hawk circling over an endless
hallucination

long ago we rode here
looking for gold
now we long for things
we don't deserve
water that does not burn our throats
sleep that does not bring madness
long nights   gray clouds   cold sand

Walking Upside Down on the Other Side of the World

Quando falamos nesta cidade perdida
when we speak in this lost city
our words bubble out of our mouths
like the *orações* / prayers of drowned children
through air so hot and green   it holds us
in suspension like bottled glass

here *perto deste grande rio* / near this great river
on the edge of this great forest of stumps
anaconda clouds glide over us like sinuous birds
and the throats of lovers fill with mud and black water

here you can get anyone killed for $50
by the *jagunços* in cowboy boots and aviator glasses
who sit in the bars nursing cold beers

here iron ore is sucked out of
the earth like blood   and a section
of bamboo filled with
gold dust will buy you a quick death

in this Anopheles democracy of sudden disasters
mosquitoes spread malaria equally to everyone
garimpeiros, *caboclos*, assassins,
colonels who ride in air conditioned cars
babies who sleep in hammocks

here the dead speak the words
the living are afraid to utter
and each kiss   given in fear
is as swift as the tongue of a bat
probing a flower

There's No Sin South of the Equator

Pull back the covers   turn off the lights
let's get high on *pango, liamba, dirijo, birra,*
elva, fininha, fumo de Angola

at sixty degrees south   cyclonic winds
swirl around the pole without ceasing
nothing stops them   not land   not remorse
not confession
nada

right now   under our bed
icebergs are being tossed like scree
by waves that carry the bones and wrecks
and broken masts of every part of us that ever went
down

below the equator
sin does not exist
but we have learned this too late

venha   come
enter the great emptiness
that encircles the world
see *the história infeliz*
the sad   history
love has ordained

Cali

do you remember how the light from the streetlamps
coated us like brown glass   how we lay
listening to the whir of the fan   the whine of mosquitoes
a bottle breaking in the street below
machinegun fire   screams   tanks rumbling past

something flared pink and orange
extravagant as a silk scarf and a chip
of cement flew over us and buried itself
in the wall half an inch from
your head

we rolled to the floor   crawled
to the bathroom   took refuge
in the shower   turned on the water
and held each other laughing
as if being together made us immortal

all night death drew shadows
on the walls   the water coiled
down the drain in the wrong direction
once I looked up and saw something
calm and terrible in your face
as if you had always known
this would happen   as if you
welcomed it

Latitude Zero

the temptation to follow pushes us forward
like a strong wind   when we flee
before a storm

when did we first see   mud-sopped rivers
littered with hammock-strung boats   cathedrals of sunken
trees circled by pink dolphins and neon-striped fish

the treasures that float up from the bottom
are always electric   carnivorous
impossible to abandon

so we have spent our lives
swimming after lost things   the scent of souls
abandoned cities   foods we can no longer buy at any price
raw sugar   foreign gods

In the Cold Lands

Here in the cold lands / *nas terras frígidas*   the fog
slides into our dreams   *nada tem uma cor brilhante*
no macaws, mangos, *onças-pintadas*, palm trees swaying
like carnival dancers

here the monsters of despair come every night   Beowulf
gripping the bloody head of Grendel's mother   seafarers who
measure their years in winters   women who have no names
given to strangers as peace offerings   wild seas
that crush the hulls of ships

here the days are short as broken sticks   and the drowned
freeze right-side up with their eyes open   *Iemanjá, Obá, Ogun,*
Xangô   onde ficam / where are   the trances of the south
the ceremonies   the *Mães de Santos*

when we bow our heads to pray   the wind is a blade
and such gods as there are   /   are indifferent as
skinning knives

Cold Snap

dying is something you only do
once

you don't have to get good at it

My Father's Leaves

when he was very old
my father told me he had lost
his leaves

he held out his hands   thin
& cold & I
took them in mine & said   your
gloves   Daddy
you lost your gloves

and thus I tracked him
& loved him
through metaphor

Fado Tropical

O *mundo do rio*   the world of the river
is not the world of the bridge   not the world
of memory   *não o mundo do passado*
not the world of the past   *não o mundo da*
saudade   not the world of longing

beneath the pollen that lacquers the surface   beneath the light
that combs the water   something indeterminate
lies in wait

o que é   what is it
that swims like a fish but is not a fish
that eats bone and flesh but has no teeth
cold-blooded, intelligent
suave como uma pantera   smooth as a panther

Leia a água
read the river

translate

A Reunião / The Conference

When I entered the hall
they filled my head with birds
macaws   parrots   chachalacas

I could feel them whistling crackling
bumping into one another behind
my sinuses   the birds sang of love & death
poetry put in cages   people
who only wrote to mimic the sounds
of their own voices   rich women
who tried to buy prizes

but I wanted to hear the sounds of the
jungle   the vast humming of sap
running through ten million trees
the slither of the *cascabel muda*
the hush of a lone dugout canoe
riding the current   the silent running
of piranhas & pink dolphins
the ancient music of hot nights
drenched and burned
in the trilling of transparent frogs

How We Lost Solange

We heard there was a price on your head
that the *jagunços* were after you because
you had occupied land you did not own
insulted the colonels
and drunk *caçhaca* with handsome slim-
hipped men young enough to be your sons

they said you
had turned into a parrot
and flown into the jungle
that your legs had been eaten off
by termites
that the Kayapó found you
wrapped you in bark
made you whole again
and fed you bitter potions concocted from
dragon's blood, milk of the *ila*, cat's claw, and *lanhuiqui*

they said you slept naked with the Kuikuro
Matipu Mehinako Nahukuá Suyá Trumai
Waura and Yawalapiti in a promiscuous pile
refusing to say whether you preferred
to have sex with women or men
because the distinction
made no sense

far up the Xingu, they said,
you reclined in a hammock
made of human finger bones
chewing on the blue gills of
phantom plecos and feeding your
lust with spicy stews made
from piranhas and spotted corys

they said that since you
left us you had drunk human blood
ascended above the canopy
on a jacaré skin
and spoken to gods so terrible
that not even the Aweti dared to look
you in the face

we formed a rescue team
and went in with helicopters
and tranquilizers hoping to get to you
before the *jagunços* did

but you saw us coming
in a dream
and left on a ribbon of water
and gold light   trailing your
long brown hair behind you like a
torn flag

in the note we found
tied to the thumb of your hammock
you told us we would
never find you
you wrote that you had taken
a jaguar for a lover
sifted your flesh
into the great oxbow lakes
where it rains black mud
cast off the flowered
husk of your body
and become a white orchid
floating on dark water

Travelers With No Ticket Home
(2014)

In Those Days Rivers Could Not Cool Me

I once lived in places
where volcanoes erupted   the water was poison
and the night swarmed with termites
that tasted like glue

there were rooms where I lay so wrapped
in fever that the fans overhead seemed ecstatic
in their whirling
rooms where I saw light the color of blood and bruised
plums   had hallucinations   dreams   terrors so great
they set me shrieking

once for 4 hours straight I spoke in rhymed couplets
and no one could make me shut up
until I threw off the sheets and ran into the tropical night
like a woman on fire

in those days   rivers could not cool me
threats could not subdue me   I burned
and burned with illness   lust   and fear
and your lightest touch seemed like a blow

later   I cooked a monkey in cream sauce
and we ate it as jungle rats ran the rafters
over our heads   the next afternoon I nearly
stepped on a nine foot fer-de-lance

only a mad woman could have loved such a life
but I did   I do   loved the strangeness of it
the non-humanness of it   the sure knowledge that death
was so small and close it could buzz in my ear

The Invisible Forests of Amapá

Crested Capuchin, Nectar Bat,
Three-toed Sloth, Golden Lion Tamarin,
Red-Handed Howling Monkey, Dark-Throated
Seedeater, Blue-Winged Macaw

great rivers veiled in steam
sixty billion trees
reaching toward a sky so green
it burns like copper

Inquisition

You ask me how I am
pecking like a yellow-tailed cuckoo
at the thin shield of green heat
that protects me from a sky that can be shredded like paper

in this land   god is a poisonous spider
the size of a shoe   a lash of fire ants
a snake with hinged fangs

above this tangled canopy of doomed trees
the clouds are writing desperately important messages
we can't read   and that log lodged in the mud behind you
is an alligator with teeth like a cross-cut saw

do not ask me how I am
do not ask me if we will survive

there are so many ways to die here
I've lost track

Chacruna Traz Luz / Chacruna Brings Light

I still have that photo of you standing on the bank
of the Juruá   naked   your hair tangled
your lips pursed in surprise   or perhaps terror

On either side of you   wearing only penis gourds
two Kashinahua (or maybe Tarauacá) are blowing
hallucinogenic snuff up your nostrils
either through hollow puma bones
or the leg bones of some small bird   now extinct
whose feathers you have woven into the wreath
you wear as a crown

on the back of the photo you wrote:
Chacruna traz luz / Chacruna brings light
Huaira, Punga Amarillo, Capirona, Lopuna Blanca,
Challucahaki, Camu camu

the head spirits are starting to speak
my body is dissolving

and then   in an almost indecipherable scrawl:
get me out of here!

After Carnival

how you loved it in the beginning
the flashing sequins   the bare thighs and breasts
the drumming that you said made you feel
as if you were being passed from hand to hand
over a crowd of 72,000 people
who loved you more than your own mother

on Ash Wednesday everyone else stopped dancing
but you went on and on   as if someone had glued
invisible red shoes to your feet

even when it started raining and your feathers drooped
like the plumage of a dying bird
even when your purple wig bled into your eyes
and the soles of your feet were bloody
with the stigmata of your martyrdom
you kept on chanting the name of Yansan
Candomblé goddess of wind and storms
merciless Yansan who rode you like a horse
and pulled on your legs and arms with invisible strings

the samba whispers terrible secrets!
you cried but you would not tell me what they were

how easy it is to give ourselves to the gods, *o meu bem*
how hard to take ourselves back

Milking the Surucucu

We stood face to face sweating
and slapping at blackflies
and fought about the best way
to milk a snake for its venom

you had just caught a *surucucu* behind the neck
nine feet long a head a handspan across
already it was coiling up your arm
as if the rainforest had come alive on your flesh

your eyes were closed   your head was back
your lips were pursed   as if waiting for a kiss

I often think of how you dreamed of death, Solange
how relentlessly you pursued it

Under the Bocurubu Trees

When the river twisted east like a streamer of honed silver
and flocks of macaws burned blue in the *bocurubu* trees
the last six speakers of *Arikapú*
walked through shadows hot as cooling iron
whispering to each other in a language that sounded
like water running over pebbles

they did not turn to look at us   standing there beside our canoes
we were the noise that had drowned their silence
the thieves who had cut out their tongues
pale ghosts in their green light
our words harsh and incomprehensible
as the ringing of axes

Onça Pintada / Painted Tiger

at night when we wake   we see Solange standing beside us
and feel *seu hálito quente /* her hot breath
on our faces

trees and vines are tattooed on her body
when she moves   they flow across her breasts and thighs
como o Rio Branco em inundação
like the Rio Solimões in flood

Solange   who stalks us by day
and watches over us by night
Solange   who is everything we have destroyed

Castanha-de-cutia, castanha-do-pará,
angelim-vermelho
the lungs of the world emptied
its rivers fouled with arsenic

Solange *a única que é tudo*
the painted tiger who pads behind us
on soft paws

Solange Encourages a River to Destroy a Dam

Xingu   Xingu
who is that dancer whirling and blind
Xingu what god rides her head

Xingu you are a *jagunço*   a *jararaca*
uma santa mulher   a holy woman
who smokes a cigar

you are the *boca da cobra*   the mouth of the snake
the soft pink part we see just before it strikes

Crown of Parrots

Among the pale columns of light
that fall from the great trees
wild pigs are swimming the river
like commuters entering a phantom city

your breath smells of *pinga*
your lips are the color of *açaí*
the forest floor beneath our feet
seethes with iridescent flies
that rise up around us in clouds like hissing stars

you are calling up the dead again
the lost ones who leave holes at our tables
chanting in that high, terrifying voice you
always used when you spoke to your mother

Seru, Guanandi, Conduru you are crying
there will be no escape
Pau-marfim, Angelim-Vermelho, Crown of Parrots

Solange, what horrors are you courting
as we stand knee-deep in flies
trapped between this black-water river
and this muddy *igarapé*

Nightingales

In the dying light   when the grapes
hung heavy   and the owls hunted   and all the small things
in the darkness did not know the names we had given them
I saw you again   reincarnated as a black horizon

saw the whipsaw of your smile   the dirt
under your fingernails   the way you threw back
your head when you laughed   your disdain
for joy

that night (and that night only)   I smelled the hot scent
of your flesh as if we still stood arguing in that forest
where once   long ago   the howler monkeys taunted us
like insane nightingales

Conquistador

on the far side of the lagoon
he rides in circles

day after day he follows the same path
searching for a way back to the mountains
where the air is cold and clear
and the snow burns his flesh like frozen iron

he came to this place to conquer it
but how do you conquer mud and water
birds so bright they burn your eyes
women who can walk through trees
men whose arrows stop your breath

once he wanted to rule a continent
now all he wants is to find
four square feet of dirt
solid enough to stand on

View from the Balcony

Nine times the sun rose over the bay
nine times the sea looked as if some great
fish had been slaughtered between
the channel and the point

in the streets people dressed in strange
brightly-colored clothing
danced to songs of drought and starvation

each night the spirit of Elizabeth Bishop
walked in the park her lover had designed
where palm trees waved like human hands
the wind was a cough that stopped and started
and the heat burned like strong coffee

from our balcony high above it all
we could see long white ships
taking people to kinder places

this is how we learned about despair
this is how we were schooled in it

Travelers With No Ticket Home

nesta cidade dos sonhos
in this city of hallucinations
the air is like *cola quente* / hot glue
and the buildings are stuck waist-deep
in asphalt *tão suave* / so soft
you can chew it like gum

over the sea the frigate birds hang motionless
parados congeladas
stopped in mid-flight like a flock of ethereal scissors

in the parks *acima da cidade*
hikers are ambushed
and robbed at gunpoint
by hungry men in rubber sandals
who flow out of a jungle thick as green glass

on some days in mid-summer
no meio do verão
when the heat seethes off the pavement
like steam   and the moon is waxing left to right
and water is swirling slowly down the drains
in the wrong direction
and the hospitals are full of
children crucified
by breakbone fever

the newly resurrected join us
and we wander the streets together
eating spoiled shrimp and drinking warm beer

The People of Brazil Discover the Portuguese

Easter, April 1, 1500

Vast blue bleeding into a gray horizon
surf choking on the rocks
something has broken through the storm clouds
that line up in the afternoon like bundles of piassava

for thousands of years we have had our canoes,
our fishing nets circling in the air
the taste of mangos in our mouths
the rocking of our hammocks
the scent of jacaranda

what is it that comes out of the east
like a tower of bones
white   with fluttering wings
larger than the largest bird we have ever seen

what new plague is the wind
blowing toward us

The Welcoming Committee

I conceive there is more barbarity in tearing a [man's] body
limb from limb by racks and torments . . . under the color of
piety and religion, than to roast and eat him after he is dead.
—Michele de Montaigne, *On Cannibals*

behind the mountains   lies another range of mountains
made of clouds   where the dead rock in hammocks
woven of snakes

and behind that lies a fire that never stops burning
and behind that still more mountains
made of a smoke that sears our lungs
like burned sugar

the air here is clear and thick as gelatin
and everything trapped in it is dead
poised forever above a sea of molten glass

we are birds with black wings
that have been sewn on our backs
by our enemies (of which we have many)

we can smell the dust on high cabinets
mites in our clothing
cats on the street eleven stories below us

our throats are made of clay
our livers are on fire
we are blind and clairvoyant

we are the Portuguese coming into Guanabara Bay
in caravels after eight months
of fucking each other and eating rats

we are fools and scoundrels
saints and sadists

we are two lovers in an apartment
enclosed in glass

we are everyone and no one

we are the Portuguese coming into Guanabara Bay
waving at the beautiful naked people on the beach
who are waiting to eat us

Malaria / Dengue / Man-Moth / Homem-traça

rains swept the streets
washing hallucinations into the sewers
on the soccer field under lights that cut the
night to shreds the games went on

you lay on a narrow cot   in a small room
drinking rum   picking at the sheets
and reciting scraps of poetry

geckos ate the mosquitoes on the walls
blackflies swarmed around the lamp
the water tasted like mold
the floors buckled gunfire rattled in the distance
and the sirens never stopped keening

just before dawn   you told me you could see stairs made of fever
don't climb them! I begged   but as always you ignored me

you're a coward   you said   *you know nothing of beauty*
Elizabeth Bishop herself is standing here
with one arm around Lota and the other around the Man-Moth

Homem-traça
Homem-traça
doesn't that mean anything to you!

then you begged me to help you
beat your hands against the sides of your cot
clawed at your eyes

The City of Apocalyptic Visions

Broken windows   stops in a giant
harmonica wailing in the hot winds that blow
up from the South   and you again in this room
with the broken lamp and the sprung bed
floating half an inch above my carpet
with your eyes closed and your lips drawn back

my love   my yellow-eyed jaguar
I am not the one who is dead
you are   and yet you return
chewing on coca leaves
drinking guarana   feeding on my
bitterness and remorse as if they were sugar

You come back unbidden to tell your endless stories
of black rivers   wild pigs   spiders big as saucers
red-eyed monkeys that fuck in the trees
better than you / better than you ever could

Solange   if you are dead
stay that way   stay in that half-forgotten jungle
that rises off my life like pale steam
don't visit me here in this city you hated
its streets   its sewers   its long hard winters
its dirt   grit   absence of stars

In the end you even hated my body
which you said had come to smell like civilization
how bitterly you said that word
as if your tongue were the tongue
of a fer-de-lance
as if everything except me
was green   tangled   too beautiful to bear

Outside the Garden / *Fora do Jardim*

onde fica where is that city with its bruised sky
endless soccer games
buildings dripping with rust and rot
air blued with the scent of bananas and mold
people who dance when there is no reason for joy

onde ficam / where are   those long nights
denseas, quentes, e úmidas
walls drenched in jasmine and piss
silent parks where bands of monkeys sleep in Jabuticaba trees
and malaria burns off the puddles like black fire

here in the cold lands the wind is blowing from the north
our gardens are dying   the earth is hardening
and naked twigs are whipping at our windows like headless snakes

Defective Instructions for Becoming a Shaman

cast off your flesh like the pelt of a molting snake   you told me
walk to the *aldeia dos mortos* / the village of the dead
where the old grow young   the young grow old
and women hunt jaguars under a snake of stars

become *um morcego*   a bat
an armadillo   a bird with a human face
não pode haver nada no mundo que não é você
there can be nothing left in the world that isn't you

you never mentioned the web that hangs between
the visible and invisible worlds
dancers who hold their eyes in their hands
the *Boitatá* who glows in the dark
the *Mapinguari* who rips the tongues from cows
the *Curupira* who eats poachers

you didn't warn me about *o túnel de espinhos*
the river of snakes   the plain of thorns
or those transparent beings with small hot hands
who would offer me a crown of Macaw feathers

now I sit here   trapped in the curare of regret
as fever eats my body like a hungry *jacaré*

Iemanjá

Afro-Brazilian Goddess of the Sea

By day the foam curls under her feet
like a carpet of broken crystals

by night she moves beneath the waves
dark-skinned mother
glowing mystery of the deepest rifts
she who climbs mountains
that have never seen the sun

in her left hand she holds a mirror
that reflects your face
as it would have appeared
if you had drowned

your eyes swimming in your head
like a pair of startled fish
your lashes trembling like seaweed
your lips wet and open
all your pain dissolved in her salty kisses

Walking toward the Largo do Machado

when the smell of jasmine
flows through the streets of Catete like a warm fog
when the scent is so liquid you can
breathe it in   get drunk and stagger
I think of all the years I have loved you
and all the years I will go on loving you
I think of how we protect each other from pain and betrayal
how each night we wrap ourselves around each other
and peace floats above our bed like a canopy of white petals

The Kama Sutra of Kindness: Position Number 1

in ancient Japan
after the first night
poems were exchanged
between lovers

a branch of white blossoms
rests against the sky
you sleep
on my blue silk sheets

the brush brings words
to the blank rice papers
you touch me
and I speak

the third time
you enter a woman
it is mandatory
to say something kind

when I smell your hair
I think of wind and anemone

the imagination has
its own erogenous zones

your body bears me
to another season
thank you for resting
here with me
balanced on the crested moon

The Kama Sutra of Kindness: Position Number 3

It's easy to love
through a cold spring
when the poles
of the willows
turn green
pollen falls like
a yellow curtain
and the scent of
Paper Whites
clots the air

but to love for a lifetime
takes talent

you have to mix yourself
with the strange
beauty of someone
else
wake each morning
for 72,000
mornings in
a row so
breathed and
bound and
tangled
that you can hardly
sort out
your arms
and legs

you have to
find forgiveness
in everything
even ink stains

and broken cups

you have be willing to move through
life
together
the way the long
grasses move
in a field
when you careen
blindly toward
the other side

there's never going to be anything
straight or predictable
about your path
except the
flattening
and the springing
back

you just go on walking for years
hand in hand
waist deep in the weeds
bent slightly forward
like two question
marks
and all the while it
burns
my dear
it burns beautifully above
you
and goes on
burning
like a relentless
sun

The Martyrdom of Carmen Miranda

If you want to look like the quintessential hoochie coochie girl, there is no better costume to have than the Ultimate Collection Carmen Miranda Outfit.
—Rubie's Costume Company, Advertisement

in that foreign land
you were always a joke
the fruit basket hats
the crippling high heels
the bare midriff
the broken English
the carnival mask smile

done up in pompoms like a pet poodle
wearing your past on the inside
like a hair shirt
the Brazilian Bombshell
who could only say *hot dog*
moneey moneey moneey
does you like me?

never mentioning
the long hours you worked in the hat shop
to buy medicine for your tubercular sister
the bad marriage to the man who beat you
the miscarriages, depression, pills
the pain you felt when at last you came home
and discovered your own people despised you
for selling out to Uncle Sam

when your gay composer protested
your betrayal of Brazil by swallowing rat poison
you danced on like a frantic puppet
singing of the Afro-Brazilian gods

in a language no one understood

Chica Chica Boom Chic
Chica Chica Boom Chic

Carmen   like you we are all travelers
who set out believing we can bring back
something to make it worth the trip
money, love, hammocks, fame
something that will make us happy and whole
something that will heal our wounds
and give us peace

Jacob's Ladder

my great aunts   hair done up in braids
calico feedsack dresses   aprons full of chicken feed
knew absolute silence   breath of a candle
hiss of a coal oil lamp   the cackle of a laying hen
but what would they have said
if I had spoken to them in Portuguese?

queridas tias / dearest aunts the jungle is thicker than corn
mais grosso do que o milho
greener than cucumbers/*mais verde do que pepinos*
filled with black lagoons that shine like obsidian

queridas tias / dearest aunts
sooner or later / *mais cedo ou mais tarde*
we all stand at the foot of a ladder that's missing rungs
speaking in tongues no one can understand

Notes

Arash's Song is written in the voice of a troubadour who travels across Neolithic Europe. He is one of the principal characters in Mary Mackey's novel *The Village of Bones: Sabalah's Tale* (New York, NY: Lowenstein Associates, 2016).

Our Lady of Dengue: Dengue fever is a mosquito-borne tropical disease. It is also known as "breakbone fever" because it causes severe joint pains.

The last two lines of *The Citizens of Pompeii Shelter in Place* come from Revelation 16:8 and 16:20. Lava Creek, Huckleberry Ridge, Yellowstone, Kasbek, Lokbatan, and Daht-Nawar are all sites of active or potentially active volcanoes.

This is Not a Poem (Do Not Mistake It for One): Vitorino Nemésio Mendes Pinheiro da Silva (1901-1978) was a poet and novelist. Professor in the Faculty of Letters at the University of Lisbon, he was best known for his novel *Mau Tempo no Canal*.

MLA: This acronym stands for The Modern Language Association of America. It is the principal professional association in the United States for scholars of language and literature. Those seeking jobs in American colleges and universities are often interviewed and hired at the MLA's annual convention.

Witness draws on the religious and legal traditions of bearing witness (or testifying) to what one has personally seen and believes to be true.

Memories of My Own Underdevelopment is set in a large Mexican city in October of 1968 a few days after the Mexican army and police forces shot and killed hundreds (some say thousands) of high school and college students and workers in Mexico City in the Plaza of Tlatelolco. The demonstrators had assembled to protest government repression, neglect of the poor, inadequate funding of education, and the armed occupation of the campus of the National Autonomous University of Mexico. The Tlatelolco massacre, which haunted the Mexican imagination for decades, took place just before Mexico hosted the Olympic Games.

The Jaguars That Prowl Our Dreams: The Rio Negro, Solimões, Tocantins, Xingu, and Javary are tributaries of the Amazon.

Sugar Zone: This poem contains references to the novel *A Primeira Mulher* by Miguel Sanches Neto.

There's No Sin South of the Equator is the English translation of the title of the song *Não existe pecado al sul do Equador* by Chico Buarque and Ruy Guerra. This poem also contains references to *Fábula Do Ribeirão do Carmo* by eighteenth century Brazilian poet Cláudio Manuel da Costa.

In The Cold Lands: Iemanjá, Obá, Ogun, and *Xangô* are Goddess and Gods of the Afro-Brazilian religion Candomblé, which is presently practiced by some 25 million people. *Mães de Santos* are the priestesses of Candomblé.

Fado Tropical: Fados are Portuguese songs about loss and longing. The word *"fado"* also means "fate." The first two lines of this poem were inspired by Maria Bethânia's "*O Mundo Do Rio Nao É O Mundo da Ponte Onde Eu Nasci Passa Um Rio.*" The phrase *"suave como uma pantera"* is a reference to Marly de Oliveira's poem *A Suave Pantera.*

The Invisible Forests of Amapá: 90 % of the total area of Brazilian state of Amapá is covered with rainforest. About 70% of this forest has not been explored by non-indigenous people and thus remains unmapped. The state of Amapá possesses the lowest rate of loss of its original vegetation of any Brazilian state, estimated in 2014 at only about 2%.

Chacruna Traz Luz / Chacruna Brings Light: Chacruna (*Psychotria viridis*) is one of the ingredients of the psychoactive drink ayahuasca (also known as yagé) used for divinatory and healing purposes by the native peoples of the Amazon. The composition of ayahuasca was first formally described in the 1950's by Harvard Ethnobotanist Richard Evans Schultes.

Under the Bocurubu Trees: As of 1998 there were only six surviving speakers of the Brazilian indigenous language *Arikapúi*.

Solange Encourages a River to Destroy a Dam: the Xingu is a 1,200 mile Brazilian river that empties into the Amazon River. Brazil is presently constructing a huge dam on the Xingu called Belo Monte. As the third-largest hydroelectric project in the world, Belo Monte will divert nearly the entire flow of the Xingu through two artificial canals leaving indigenous communities without water, fish, or means of river transport. Protests against Belo Monte are on-going. A *jararaca* is a large, poisonous pit viper. *Jagunço* is a one of 25 Brazilian Portuguese words for "hitman."

Malaria / Dengue / Man-Moth / Homen-traça: this poem contains references to Elizabeth Bishop's poem *The Man-Moth*.

Defective Instructions for Becoming a Shaman: a *jacaré*, also known as a caiman, is the Amazonian equivalent of an alligator.

Jacob's Ladder: Jacob's Ladder is a traditional quilt pattern. It is also the ladder to heaven the biblical Jacob dreams about as described in *Genesis* 28: 10-19.

Acknowledgments

Thanks to Thomas Fink whose insightful editorial suggestions were invaluable and to Sandy McIntosh and designer Heather Wood who worked tirelessly to prepare *Jaguars* for publication. I am also grateful to Pamela Berkman and Dorothy Hearst who gave me companionship, support, and critical feedback and to the members of the WELL Writers Conference and The Women's National Book Association, San Francisco Chapter; The Organization for Tropical Studies; The Virginia Center for the Creative Arts; and my late tutor, William Nestrick, who first exposed me to the French Surrealist poets. Thanks also to Jane Hirshfield, Alta Gerrey, B.L. Kennedy, Marge Piercy, Eugene Redmond, Lise Sedrez, Janine Canan, Lynda Koolish, Maxine Hong Kingston, D. Nurkse, and Al Young. I will be forever grateful to the late Richard Evans Schultes, Harvard Professor and father of modern Ethnobotany, who allowed me to audit his classes where, as an eighteen-year-old sophomore, I fell in love with the beauty and mystery of the tropics. I am also indebted to Isabel Allende who first suggested I write about my Kentucky relatives.

Finally, I would like to thank my husband Angus Wright for his unfailing affection, encouragement and support for well over thirty years, and for bidding me get up from my computer, go outside, and take walks along the American River, where every day I can see firsthand the beauty of the real world.

I also wish to express my gratitude to the editors of the periodicals and anthologies in which some of the poems in this collection first appeared:

The Careless Embrace of the Boneshaker (great weather for MEDIA); *The Cortland Review; Marsh Hawk Review; The Understanding Between Foxes and Light* (great weather for MEDIA); *Sparring With Beatnik Ghosts; Fightin' Words; Poetry Flash; Plume Poetry; Catamaran Literary Reader; Gargoyle Magazine; Spillway Magazine; Drum Voices Revue; We'Moon; Mad Hatter's Review; Entering The Real World: VCCA Poets on Mt. San Angelo 40th Anniversary Poetry Anthology; Rufous City Review; Calaveras Station Literary Journal; caRamSutra; The Women's Writing Salon; Words Upon Waters; Hastings Street; Louis Liard; So Luminous The Wild Flowers; Tebot Bach Anthology of California Poets; Tule Review; Poetry Now; Bay Crossings; The Sacramento Anthology: One Hundred Poems; The New Now Now New Millennium Turn-on Anthology; Switched-on Gutenberg; The Land Report; Life Prayers; Yellow Silk; Poetry USA; Hers; She Rises Like the Sun: Invocations of the Goddess by Contemporary American Women Poets; Women Poet: The West II; Ain't I A Woman; Down Deep; Landing Signals; MS Magazine; Networks: An Anthology of San Francisco Bay Area Women Poets; American Spectacles; Countrywomen; Plowman; Change; Women's Perspectives; Rough Times; The New Women's Survival Sourcebook; Echoes; Chili; Women Studies Newsletter; Liberation; A Fine Frenzy: Enduring Themes in Poetry; Libra; Matrix; Velvet Glove.*

And special thanks to all those who helped nourish and propagate the flowering of women's literature from the late 1960's through the 1980's by recognizing the importance of women's writing and founding magazines, journals, independent bookstores, and small presses, often at great personal expense and sacrifice.

Much of the soul of American poetry lives in its small presses and independent bookstores. Without them our lives would be poorer indeed.

About the Author

MARY MACKEY is the author of seven previous collections of poetry including *Sugar Zone* (Marsh Hawk Press, 2011) winner of the 2012 PEN Oakland Josephine Miles Award for Excellence in Literature and Finalist for the Northern California Book Awards. Her poems have appeared in numerous magazines, journals, and anthologies; been featured on *The Writers Almanac*; and been praised by Wendell Berry, Jane Hirshfield, Dennis Nurkse, Maxine Hong Kingston, Al Young, and Marge Piercy for their beauty, precision, originality, and extraordinary range.

She is also the author of fourteen novels, one of which made *The New York Times* Best Seller list. As far as anyone has been able to determine, her first novel, *Immersion* (Shameless Hussy Press, 1972), was the first novel in the world published by a Second Wave Feminist press.

Mackey's works have been translated into twelve foreign languages including Japanese, Hebrew, Russian, Greek, and Finnish. She is past president of the West Coast branch of PEN, a Fellow of the Virginia Center for the Creative Arts, a member of the National Book Critics Circle, and Professor Emeritus of English at California State University, Sacramento. For over twenty-five years she has been traveling to Brazil with her husband, Angus Wright, who writes about land reform and environmental issues.

To contact her, sample more of her work, read her blog interview series *People Who Make Books Happen*, and receive her quarterly newsletter, you are invited to visit her website at www.marymackey.com. You can also follow her on Twitter at @MMackeyAuthor and find her on Facebook at www.facebook.com/marymackeywriter. Her books are available in hard copy and as well as in e-book and Audible editions.

Mary Mackey's literary papers are archived in the Sophia Smith Special Collections Library, Smith College, Northampton, MA. Her collection of rare editions of small press poetry books is archived in the Smith College Mortimer Rare Book Collection.

TITLES FROM MARSH HAWK PRESS

Jane Augustine *Arbor Vitae; KRAZY: Visual Poems and Performance Scripts; Night Lights; A Woman's Guide to Mountain Climbing*
Tom Beckett *Dipstick (Diptych)*
Sigman Byrd *Under the Wanderer's Star*
Patricia Carlin *Original Green; Quantum Jitters; Second Nature*
Claudia Carlson *The Elephant House; My Chocolate Sarcophagus; Pocket Park*
Meredith Cole *Miniatures*
Jon Curley *Hybrid Moments; Scorch Marks*
Neil de la Flor *Almost Dorothy; An Elephant's Memory of Blizzards*
Chard deNiord *Sharp Golden Thorn*
Sharon Dolin *Serious Pink*
Steve Fellner *Blind Date with Cavafy; The Weary World Rejoices*
Thomas Fink *Selected Poems & Poetic Series; Joyride; Peace Conference; Clarity and Other Poems; After Taxes; Gossip: A Book of Poems*
Norman Finkelstein *Inside the Ghost Factory; Passing Over*
Edward Foster *The Beginning of Sorrows; Dire Straits; Mahrem: Things Men Should Do for Men; Sewing the Wind; What He Ought to Know*
Paolo Javier *The Feeling is Actual*
Burt Kimmelman *Abandoned Angel; Somehow*

Burt Kimmelman and Fred Caruso *The Pond at Cape May Point*
Basil King *The Spoken Word / The Painted Hand from Learning to Draw / A History; 77 Beasts: Basil King's Beastiary; Mirage*
Martha King *Imperfect Fit*
Phillip Lopate *At the End of the Day: Selected Poems and An Introductory Essay*
Mary Mackey *Breaking the Fever; The Jaguars That Prowl Our Dreams; Sugar Zone; Travelers With No Ticket Home*
Jason McCall *Dear Hero,*
Sandy McIntosh *A Hole In the Ocean: A Hamptons' Apprenticeship; The After-Death History of My Mother; Between Earth and Sky; Cemetery Chess: Selected and New Poems; Ernesta, in the Style of the Flamenco; Forty-Nine Guaranteed Ways to Escape Death; Obsessional: Poetry for Performance*
Stephen Paul Miller *Any Lie You Tell Will Be the Truth; The Bee Flies in May; Fort Dad; Skinny Eighth Avenue; There's Only One God and You're Not It*
Daniel Morris *Bryce Passage; Hit Play; If Not for the Courage*
Geoffrey O'Brien *The Blue Hill*
Sharon Olinka *The Good City*
Christina Olivares *No Map of the Earth Includes Stars*
Justin Petropoulos *Eminent Domain*

Paul Pines *Charlotte Songs; Divine Madness; Gathering Sparks; Last Call at the Tin Palace*
Jacquelyn Pope *Watermark*
George Quasha *Things Done for Themselves*
Karin Randolph *Either She Was*
Rochelle Ratner *Balancing Acts; Ben Casey Days; House and Home*
Michael Rerick *In Ways Impossible to Fold*
Corrine Robins *Facing It: New and Selected Poems; One Thousand Years; Today's Menu*
Eileen R. Tabios *The Connoisseur of Alleys; I Take Thee, English, for My Beloved; The Light Sang as It Left Your Eyes: Our Autobiography; Reproductions of the Empty Flagpole; Sun Stigmata; The Thorn Rosary: Selected Prose Poems and New (1998–2010)*
Eileen R. Tabios and j/j hastain *The Relational Elations of Orphaned Algebra*
Susan Terris *Ghost of Yesterday; Natural Defenses*
Madeline Tiger *Birds of Sorrow and Joy*
Tana Jean Welch *Latest Volcano*
Harriet Zinnes *Drawing on the Wall; Light Light or the Curvature of the Earth; New and Selected Poems; Weather Is Whether; Whither Nonstopping* .

ARTISTIC ADVISORY BOARD

For more information, please go to: www.marshhawkpress.org .